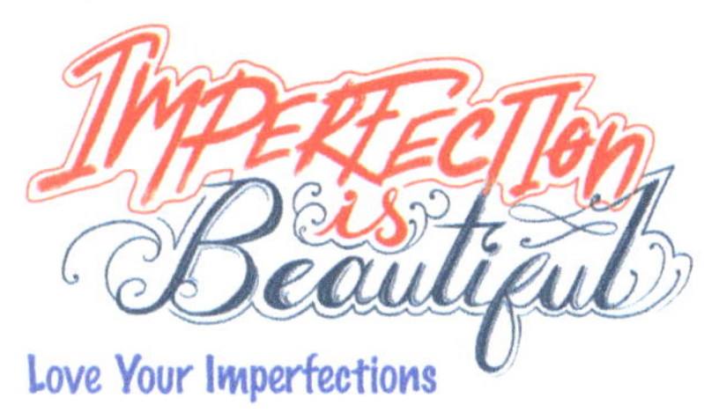

PAINTING THE

Path

OF MY

Life

Lisa MacDonald

Printed in the United States of America
Published in Hellertown, PA

Cover design by Crystal Hunter-Jones

ISBN 978-1-958711-87-3

For more information or to place bulk orders, contact the author
or Jennifer@BrightCommunications.net.

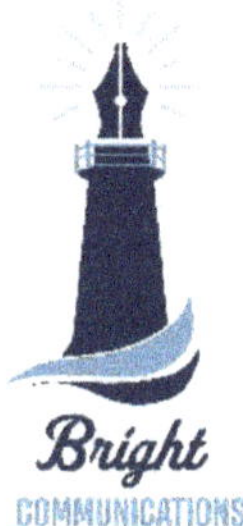

To my parents, Richard and Belkys MacDonald, and my loving boyfriend,
Zane Landis, who all have supported me and allow me to keep pushing through
to follow my dreams as an artist

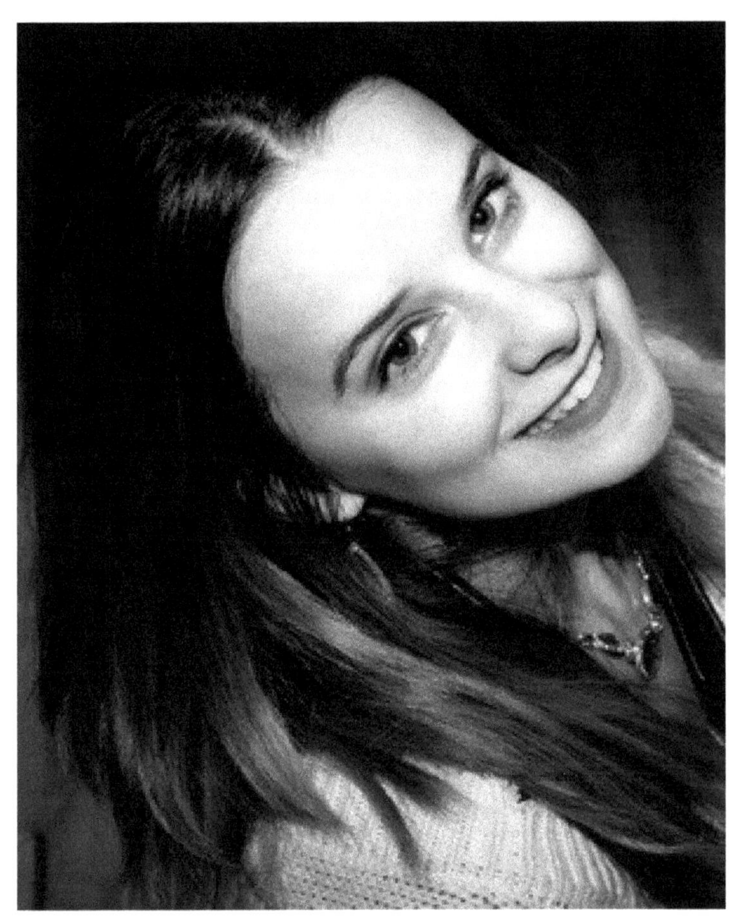

About Lisa MacDonald

Abstract Motivational Artist

I have been creating art since I was six years old. I have always enjoyed using a lot of vibrant colors because I feel colors make up happiness.

During my school years, it was difficult to make friends because I was very different and also because I didn't want to be like anybody else. I have a learning disability, which makes it hard for me to understand complex subjects and engage in different classes.

Also, I am half Dominican. I speak both Spanish and English. Sometimes I mix up my words together, and the students would make fun of me. Because of how they treated me, I felt I wasn't good at anything, and that I was not as smart as the average students. Even though school was hard and the classes weren't engaging for me, I found that I am good at art. It's where I can be free. Art has shown me ways to be confident with myself. It taught me that I can do anything I put my mind to. Also, art distracts me from my disabilities.

My artwork defines who I am and what I do. I design my artwork in an abstract form because I believe it gives my art pieces an imperfect yet beautiful view. The imperfection in my artwork symbolizes all of our own human imperfections. I want to include the true meaning of imperfections into my artwork to spread this awareness to others who are struggling to accept their own imperfections.

I want to give people the hope and the love they may be searching for.

Each piece I create has a meaning to me as an artist. Sharing that meaning is the most important, rewarding part of what I do. I believe my artwork especially connects to people who need positivity and motivation in their lives.

I believe my art and I have a powerful message to display and to speak for people in our world. All these aspects combined to make me become an Abstract Motivational Artist.

As an Abstract Motivational Artist, my goal is to spread positivity and motivation. I want my artwork and my voice to make a difference in our world. I want my artwork to help people feel connected and motivated when going through life struggles. I want my positive mindset to speak out to the world and change people's lives. Finally, I want to provide awareness through my work and my voice to help our community to be in a better place.

Acknowledgments

Thank you to all who have supported me through my journey.

I want to thank my two brothers, William and Lusinky, for encouraging me to follow my dreams as an artist.

I want to thank my mom, Belkys MacDonald, and my dad, Rich MacDonald, for their support and patience for me and my journey. I want to thank my boyfriend, Zane Landis, for being a positive influence in my life and helping me overcome all the struggles I have gone through.

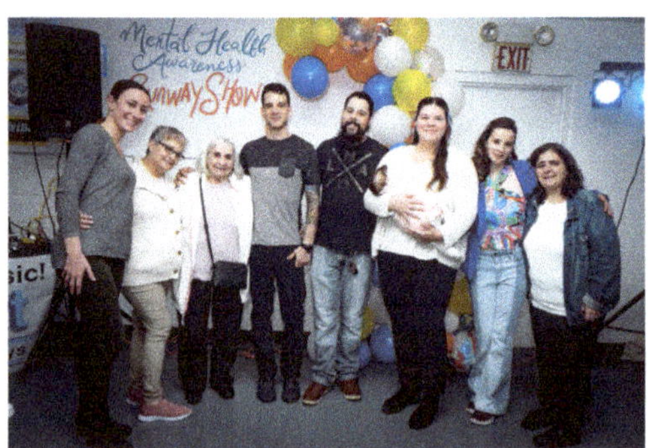
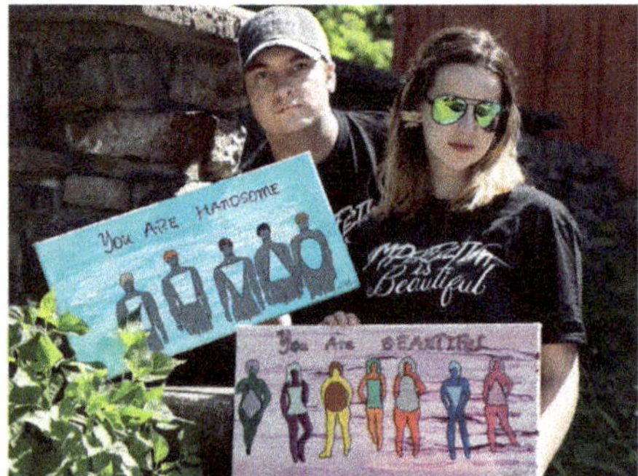
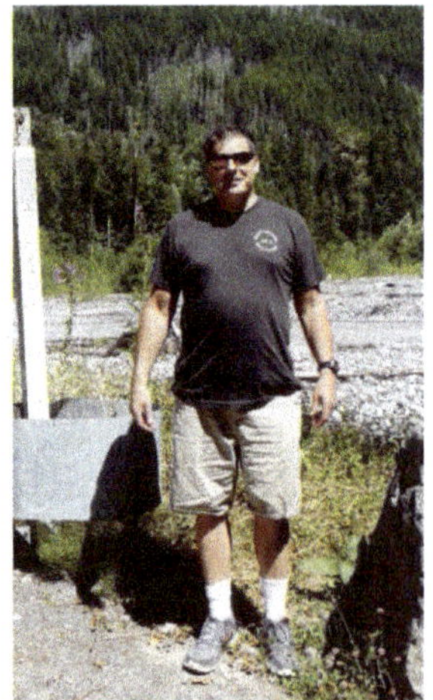

Finally, I want to thank all my supporters who are true to me for always believing in me!

About the Editor

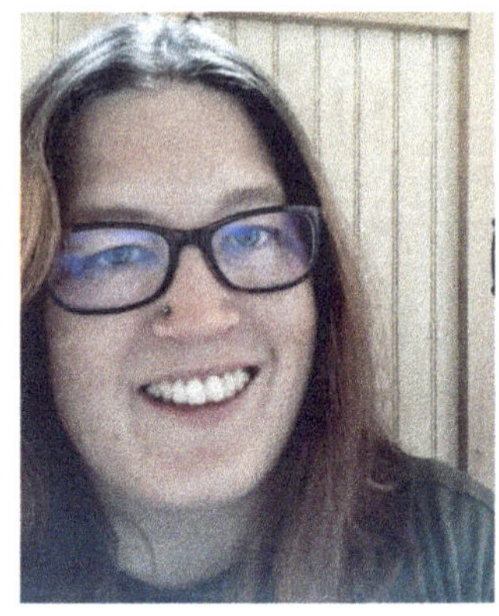

Rachael Goetzke-Hughes earned her Master of Fine Arts in Creative Writing from Wilkes University. Her memoir, *Us Girls: My Life Without a Uterus*, was published by Big Table Publishing in 2018. She loves art, cats, and Pearl Jam. She said that working on this project was an honor. She blogs about everything music and writing at http://kindalikeapoet.wordpress.com. You can learn more about her and her memoir at https://rachaeljhughes.wixsite.com/shewritesforyou.

About the Graphic Designer

Crystal Hunter-Jones graduated from Kutztown University of Pennsylvania in 2019. Specializing in graphic design, she has garnered recognition for her work on diverse projects, ranging from logos to web design. Crystal's dedication to visual excellence has set her on a path of artistic success and innovation.
Contact her for more information Crystalhunterjones@gmail.com.

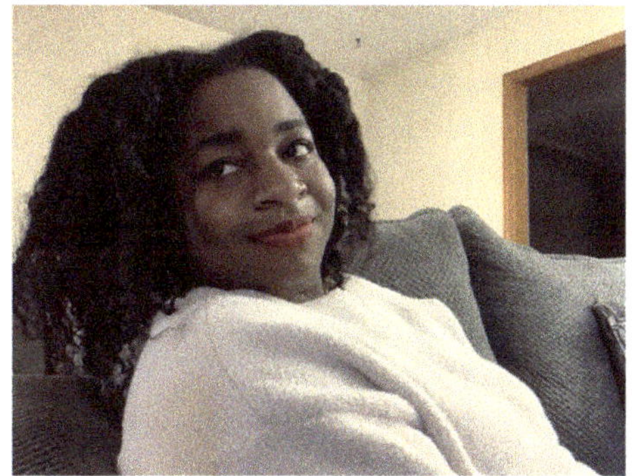

About the Photographers

Mike Robinson took the photos of the art and author. Mike has been a professional photographer for more than 30 years. His adventures in this art form have taken him to the open oceans on great sailing ships, repelling off 200-foot buildings, and capturing the tears of a bride and groom on their wedding day. The camera has pathed a wonderful life of capturing the hearts, beauty, and emotions of all he has photographed.

Learn more on what he does mike@mikerobinsonproductions.com.

Lauren Strickland is a uniquely skilled photographer with an associate's degree in photography and technology who graduated from Institute of Photography and Graphic Design. Lauren took the photos of each painting.

Follow her on Facebook to see unique and beautiful nature images https://www.facebook.com/LaurenJonesProphotography.

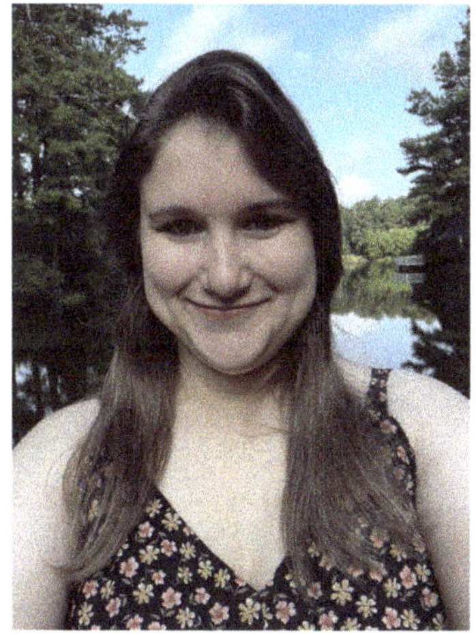

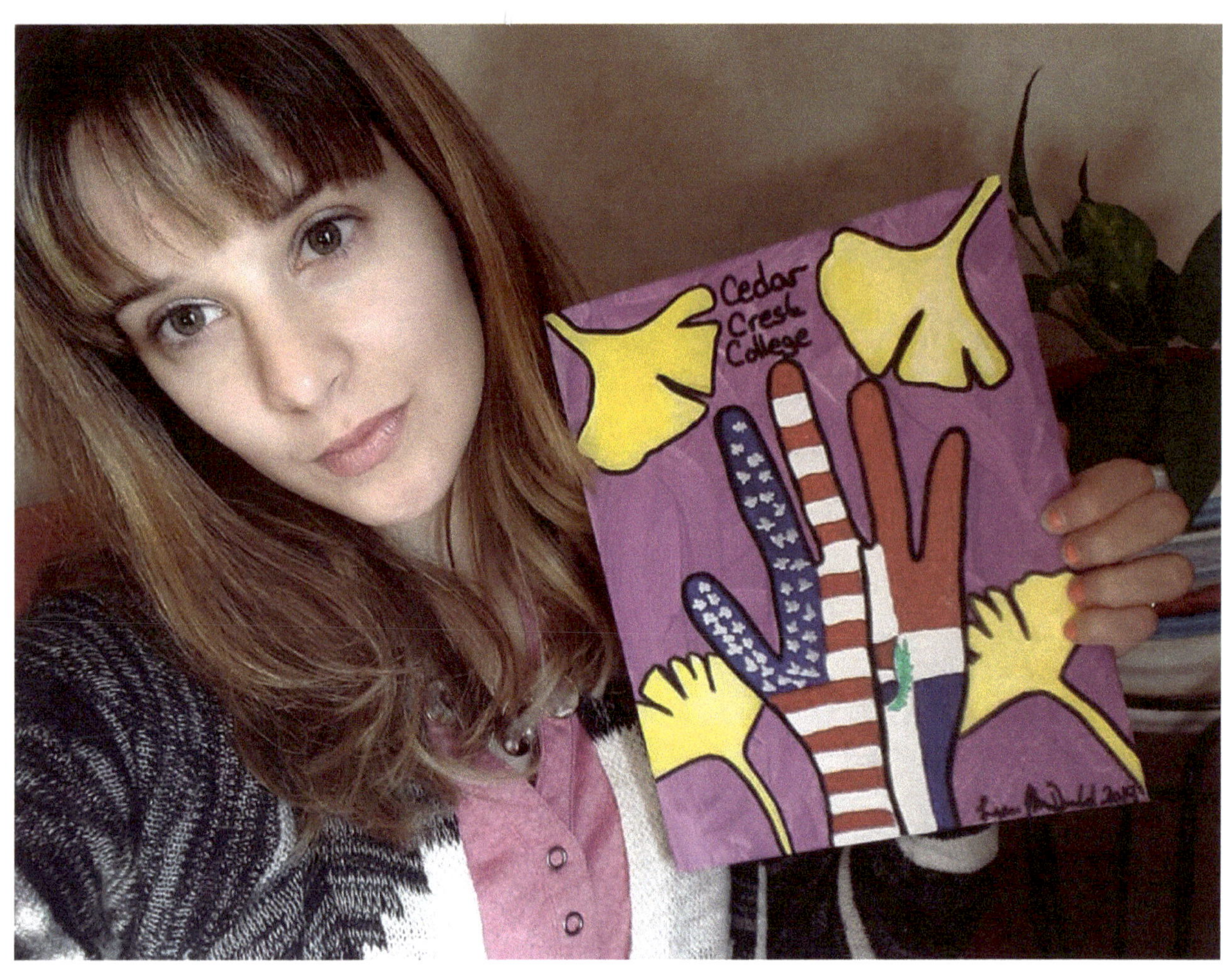

Cedar
Crest
College

I Am Half Dominican

2019

I grew up in a mixed-race family. My mother is from Dominican Republic, and my father is from Pennsylvania and is Pennsylvania Dutch (German). They both spoke different languages to me, so my entire life I've spoken Spanglish. My mother can speak English, but she felt it was important for her children to know two languages, as well as learn about Dominican Republic culture, foods, and lifestyle. My mom would take me and my brother William to Dominican Republic to visit our extended family of which I have so many: uncles, aunts, and lots and lots of cousins.

I always enjoyed my time in Dominican Republic and feeling so connected to the people, the culture, and of course, the food. It was such a blessing to meet everybody and feel accepted in that country. Everybody in Dominican Republic embraced my brother and me, and they treated us like we belonged there.

It was a such a humbling experience seeing how different their lifestyle is compared to what we have in America. We sure are spoiled.

Seeing poverty-stricken areas in Dominican Republic was devastating to me. I saw shacks, mothers washing clothes by hand, and kids playing with rocks and sticks as their toys. It really opened my eyes to a whole new perspective of my life, how much stuff I have at home, and how most Americans have it so easy. It made me want to donate my clothes, toys, and jewelry to Dominican Republic.

I remember after my sweet sixteen birthday party, my mom donated the huge, puffy, lavender dress that I wore only once for that party to a young girl in Dominican Republic. She was preparing to celebrate her *quincera* (sweet fifteenth) birthday party, which is a Dominican tradition. Doing this means a girl entering to adulthood and showcasing her purity and readiness for marriage.

When I saw that girl put on that dress, I cried at how her beautiful tan skin glowed. It gave me so much happiness to know that she got a perfect dress for her special day.

In my hometown in Pennsylvania, people discriminated against me so much that I lost my identity. I felt like I didn't even know myself. Although it hurts, I didn't let that stop me. I expressed myself through art. Now, I show myself to the community by expressing confidently that I am bilingual and half Dominican. People need to be more open-minded and accept that the fact is: In America, we are all mixed-race, and we are all unique!

I painted this hand because I wanted to represent that I am half American and half Dominican. This painting was made for the college I was attending, which was hosting a workshop at Cedar Crest College called "Express Your Nationality through Art." It was a way for others to create art, connect, be-opened minded, and learn from one another.

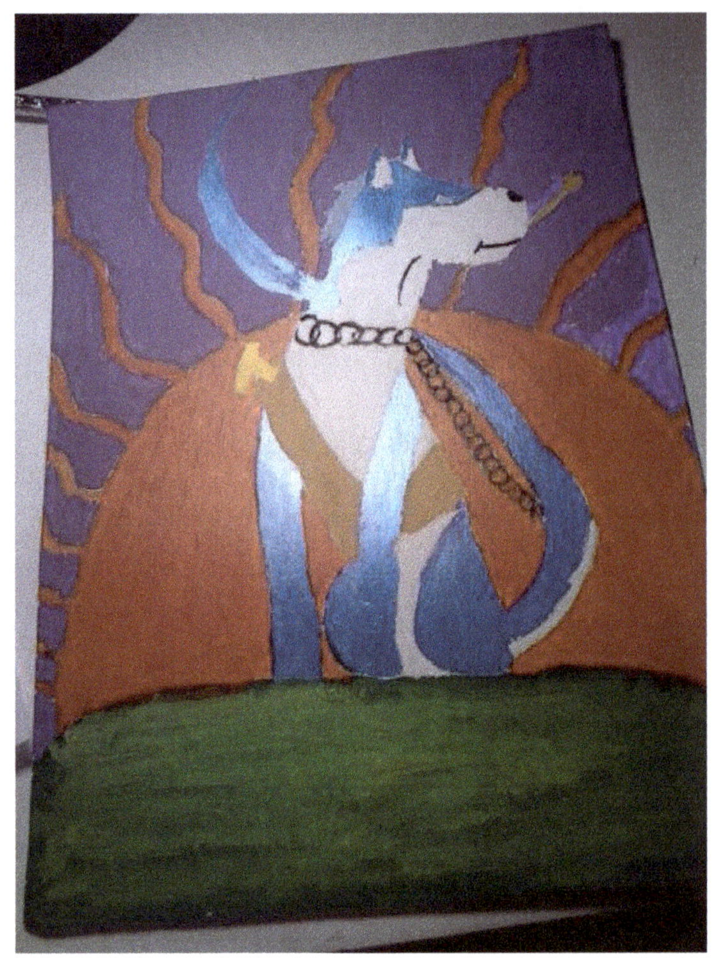

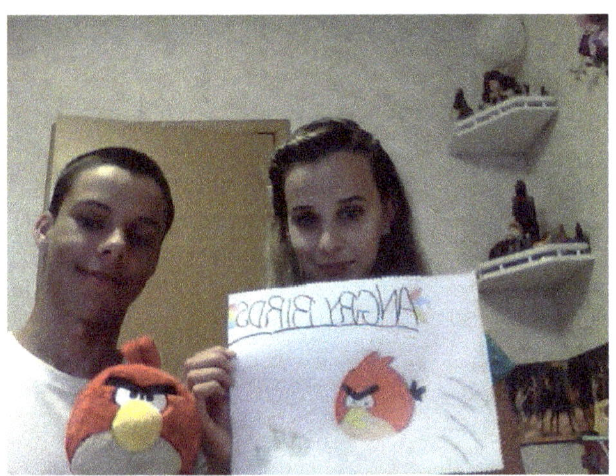

ANGRY BIRDS

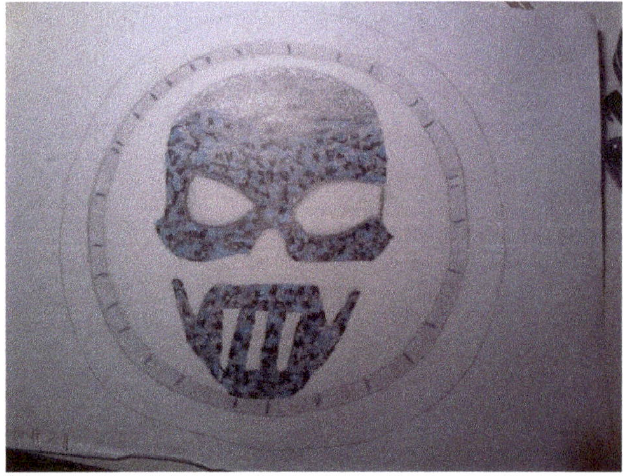

My Supporter
2006

Growing up, I always loved to draw and do crafts. It was my escape from school and my troubles learning different subjects. It was hard making friends, especially girls because they always wanted to fight me and to tear me down. So instead of making friends with girls, I just learned to be friends with myself and with my art.

My brother, William, was always there to give me ideas and inspirations to draw. I always look up to him because he knows what's best for me, and he motivates me to see more in my art. Every time he would play a new video game, he would ask me to draw a character or logo. I got excited and wanted to do my best to impress him with my amazing work. His friends also gave me ideas and suggestions on what other things I can draw. William always taught me to be strong, to not let others put me down, and to focus on what makes me happy.

When William and I were teenagers, Facebook was becoming huge. He recommended that I create a Facebook account to get my art out there. In 2010, I created a Facebook account and put all my drawings and paintings online. I got amazing comments from people, and it made me smile to see how much exposure I got. I was excited to tell William about all the exposure and how thankful I was for him recommending me to do this.

Growing up, William was not only my brother, but he was my only friend that I could trust and feel safe around. He was my number one supporter. Because of him, I started becoming the Abstract Motivational Artist that I am today.

As an adult, still pursuing my childhood dream, it is such a blessing to know that I always have both of my brothers supporting me: William and Lusinky. I grew up with Lusinky, but we are twelve years apart, and we didn't get close until my late teens. Having that positive support from both is the best feeling ever.

I sometimes feel uncomfortable talking with them about my art because I have such a different lifestyle than them. They both are married with children and are living their best lives. Although I am living my childhood dream, I'm often unsure where I belong in this average world. My brothers never judge me on my lifestyle. They always want to know what is my next move. I am forever grateful for my brothers, and I am always there for them because they have always been there for me.

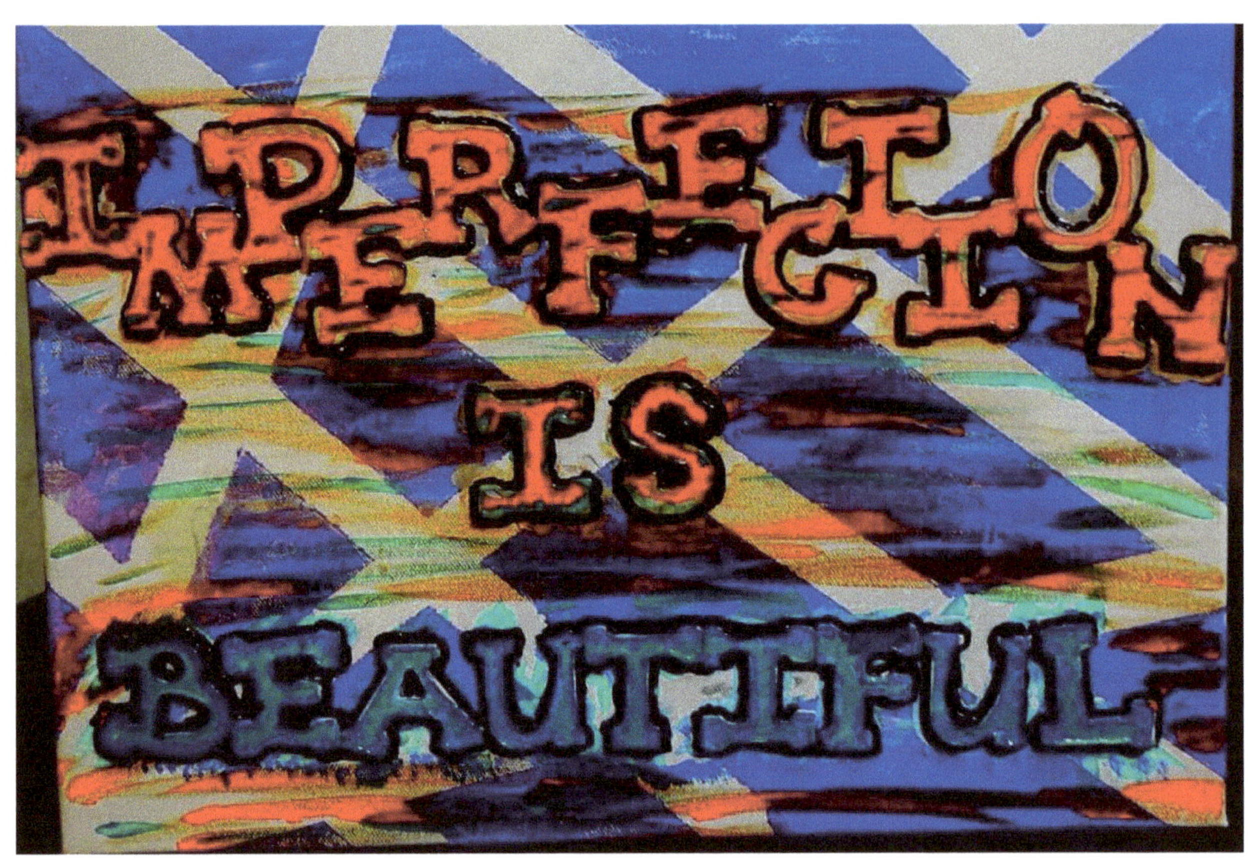

Imperfection Is Beautiful

2017

"Imperfection Is Beautiful" is an art logo for my social media: Facebook, Instagram, and YouTube. My art and myself are all made of imperfections. My art has many mistakes, and I make those mistakes into something beautiful. The mistakes are a way for me to think critically about how I can make it work.

For me, I am starting to accept all my imperfections, which includes my acne, hair, and nails—basically everything that is a struggle for any young woman. I believe my natural beauty makes me feel so deeply beautiful—despite all my imperfections.

I see myself as an artist and also as a work of art. I am still developing in this real world. My mind is full of creative ideas that deserve to be known and heard. Art has been in my life for so long that my style resembles my own artwork.

My fashion style is also very unique, with fun colors and patterns like my artwork. I like to add layers of clothing because I like the way the clothes flow onto my body, just like how paint flows onto the canvas. I always love to wear colors because it describes my personality and my art. As well, I like to wear handmade jewelry because I like to wear something different and the more unique an object is, the more it represents me and my work of art.

Likewise, I love to create abstract work because I believe abstract art is calming and emotion-evoking. This art logo *"Imperfection is Beautiful"* has helped me to find self-acceptance, and it has provided me with a better life. I hope it will encourage others to do the same. Thanks to art, my life is so complete—even with all the imperfection and beauty that's in it. I am happy to live that way!

The biggest reason why I have gotten into this is because of my difficult experience through bullying. In school, I never felt I was good enough. I went through an especially difficult time in 2014 and 2015. But in 2015, I was shown that I have beautiful purpose. My boyfriend, Zane, and I went to a couples' massage and Reiki for Valentine's Day, and it was the best feeling I have ever had. I didn't want to say just thank you. I wanted to express this gratitude through art, so I painted the business's logo and give it to a wonderful lady name Deb in person.

In her thank you letter, she told me that she loved and cherished it so much, and that it motivated her to open her own practice in 2016 called Soul Body: www.massagebook.com/Allentown~Massage~SoulBodyHealingArts.

That thank you letter completely changed my life. It made me believe that I can make something out of my art and show the world that my art has a purpose! I launched my business *Imperfection is Beautiful* in March 2017.

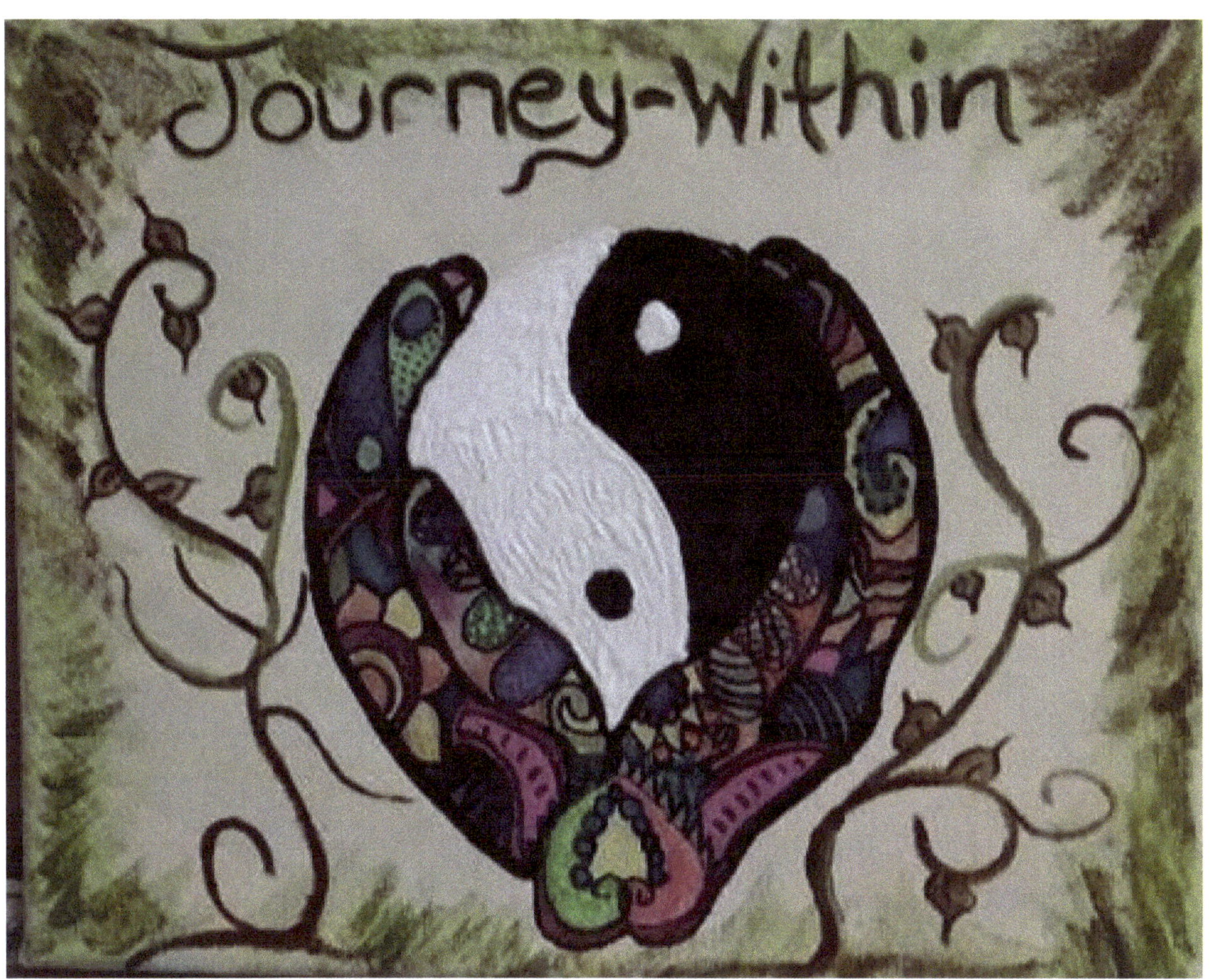

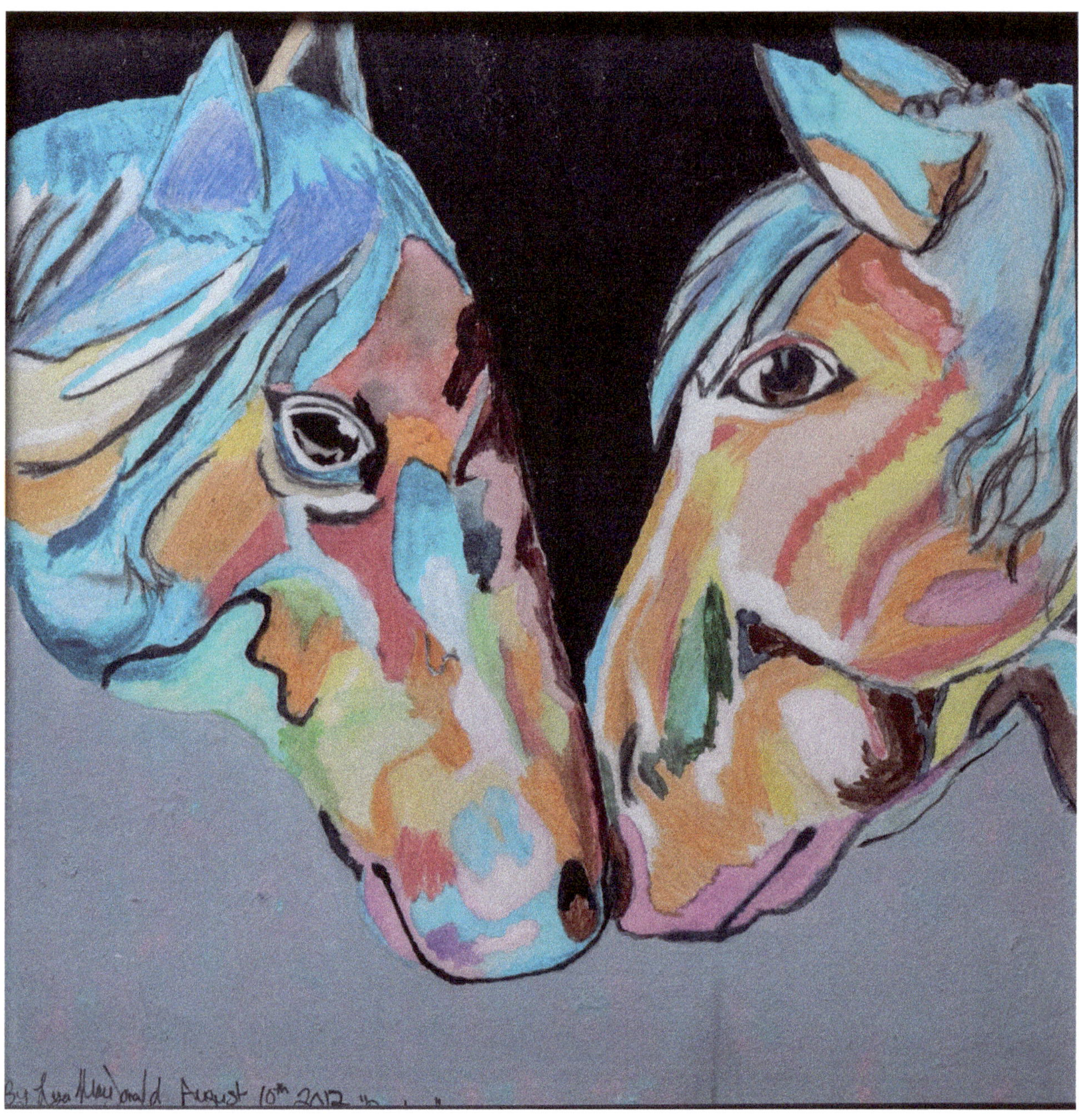

By Lisa MacDonald August 10th 2012

Vibrations of Colors

August 2012

Since I was a little girl, I have always loved horses. I really wanted to embrace the colors and the abstract forms on these horses' heads.

In 2012, when I was in high school, I couldn't resist two colorful horses in love. I loved to let my imagination run wild, adding interesting texture, lining, shapes, and colors into this painting. I used different art materials, including crayons, watercolor, acrylics, and colored pencils.

Around that year, I wanted to work on my own art pieces instead of the school art pieces and to capture my feelings by using different tones of colors to express how I felt. All these colors represent happiness and love. You can see imperfections in the way I designed these two horse heads.

Also in 2012, I met Zane. For the first time, I felt I could be myself with no judgment and just do what I love to do. He made me feel that I can truly be myself because prior to meeting Zane, I always felt judged based on the ideas I had, the clothes I wore, and the artwork I created. I never let my work truly show in school because I was afraid that somebody would hate on it and tell me that my work wasn't good enough. Even though I thought my work could mean something in the world, I was too scared to show it.

But after meeting Zane, he allowed me to keep getting my work out there. Today, looking at these two horses, I imagine my love beside me, giving me a gentle push to let the world know my name and art—no matter how wild the style and colors are. Today, I let my love of abstractions guide me to keep moving forward, to keep creating.

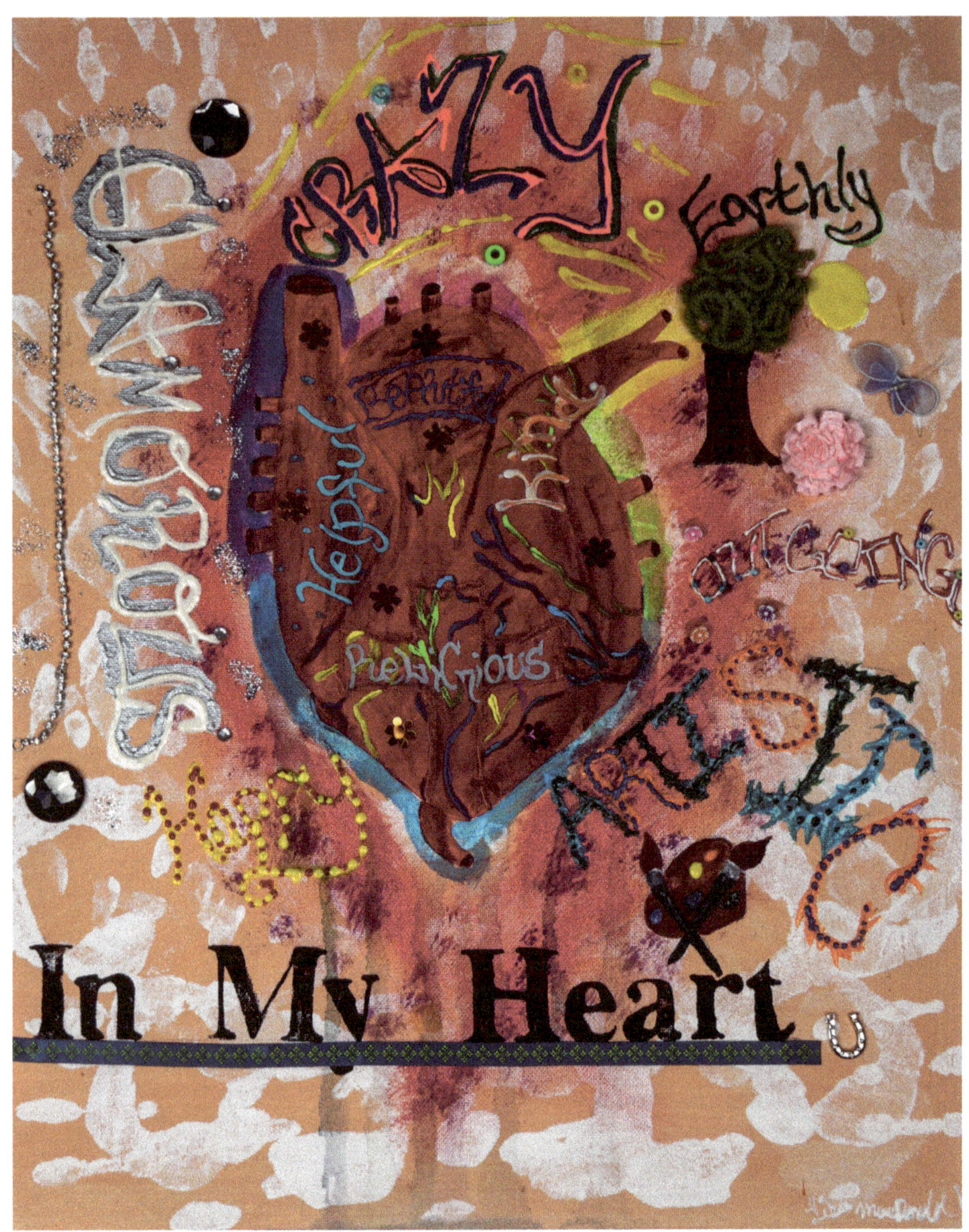

CRAZY
Earthly
GLAMOROUS
Helpful
Kind
Religious
OUTGOING
ARTISTIC
In My Heart

In My Heart

2014

I have a huge heart filled with kindness for all of the people in the world. No matter what a person does to me, I always do everything to keep passing kindness.

I also am very helpful, and I push others to find the light for which they have been searching for so long. I cherish every moment helping others, making a difference in their lives.

I am forever grateful for what I have and where I am in life. I have a great support group. I want to give the people pieces of myself so they can live life simply and blissfully.

Because I was brought up in a positive environment, I have a positive outlook on life. I want to give back by giving my love and attention to other people and make them feel special. I want to show them that they matter, that they are worthy of living here on Earth.

Showing my kindness and helpfulness creates the inner beauty I have within my heart. I feel beautiful inside because I do beautiful things for people. The feeling of beauty that is under the skin and inside the heart is true human beauty.

I also follow my spiritual side with crystals. I practice my faith by praying for myself and for others and writing in my journal for God. I believe practicing what I believe in gives me guidance and structure in my life.

I enjoy being around people. I love to talk to them, really learn about them. I believe it is important to communicate and express our thoughts and feelings because people thrive on communication. It makes us feel healthy to release and let go of tension.

Personally, to maintain my happiness, I don't let anything stop me and my happiness. Life can be very challenging, but I always tell myself that I can work this out and make things happen. Don't get me wrong: I can get down, but not for long. Every day is brand new, an opportunity when I can pick myself back up and bring out the light within me.

On especially good days, I enjoy crazy moments where I do and say funny things. I don't hide my personality. What's the point of living if you're hiding yourself? I show people the real me, which at times can be crazy, depending on my mood. I love to joke and make a fool out of myself because I love to see people laugh and have a good time. Laughter is amazing for the soul.

These characteristics of my heart make me Lisa MacDonald. They're why I will always keep following my heart.

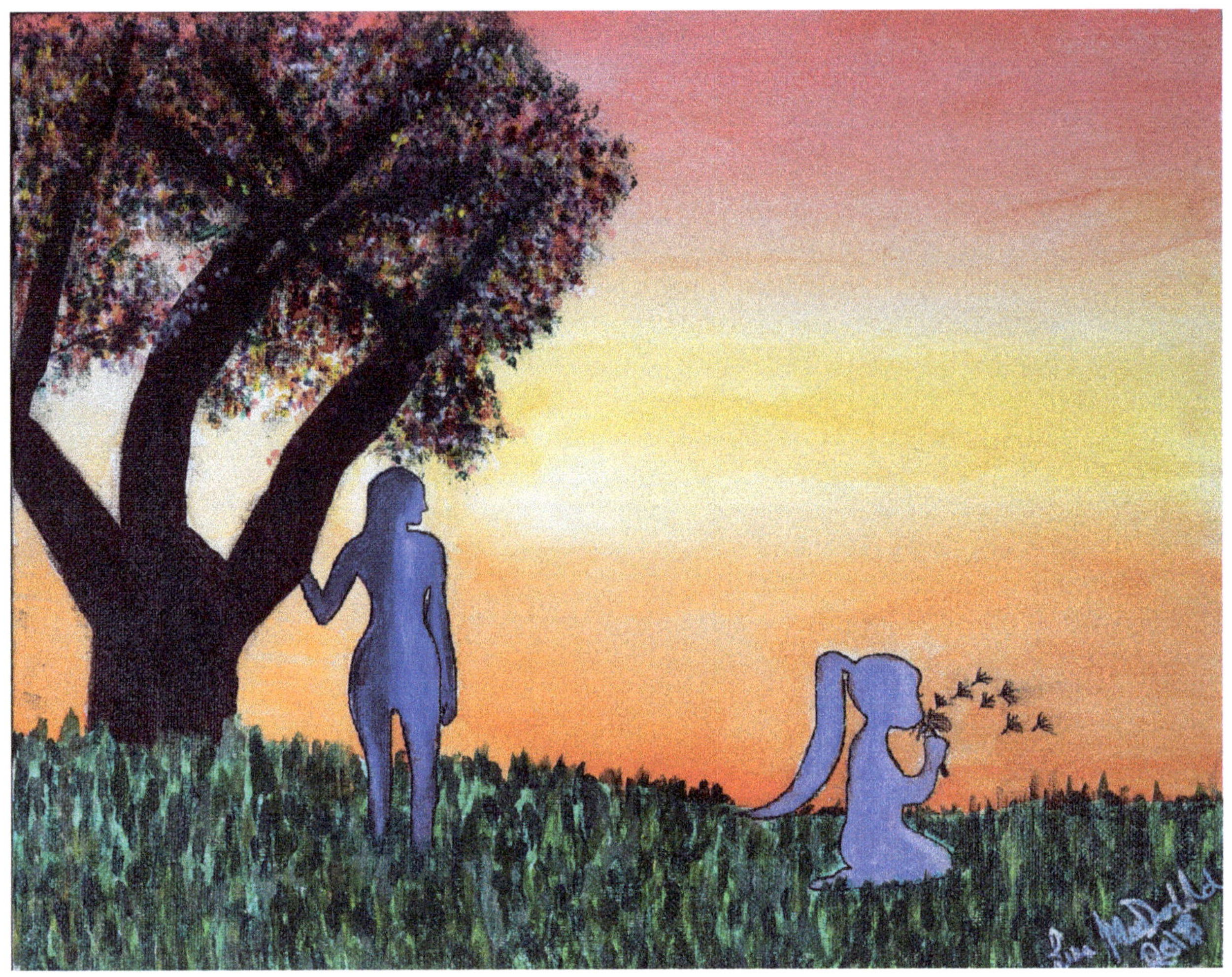

The Scent of My Childhood Life
January 2018

In this painting, I am envisioning myself as a little girl playing outside of my grandma's house.

The smells of nature—trees, grass, flowers, and the wind—bring back good memories of when I was a little girl. I enjoyed my childhood when I was outside and being free with nature. Everything seemed so pure and so fun.

In late spring and early summer, I enjoy lying on the grass, feeling the sun on my face, and hearing the soothing sounds of the birds singing. I've always been a huge fan of being outside, watching insects, picking grass, and gathering sticks.

Now as a grown woman, I miss the carefree times that I had in nature as a child. This stressful world can be so overwhelming. Being an adult in general is so overwhelming.

Sometimes on a tough day, I enjoy meditating on the grass to gain back those good times. Thinking back on my childhood memories helps me appreciate my life, my family, and myself.

No matter how old I get, I will always keep my childhood memories close to my heart and embrace my inner child. Nature made me create this beautiful piece of artwork to look at every day and every night to remind myself how amazing and peaceful my childhood was.

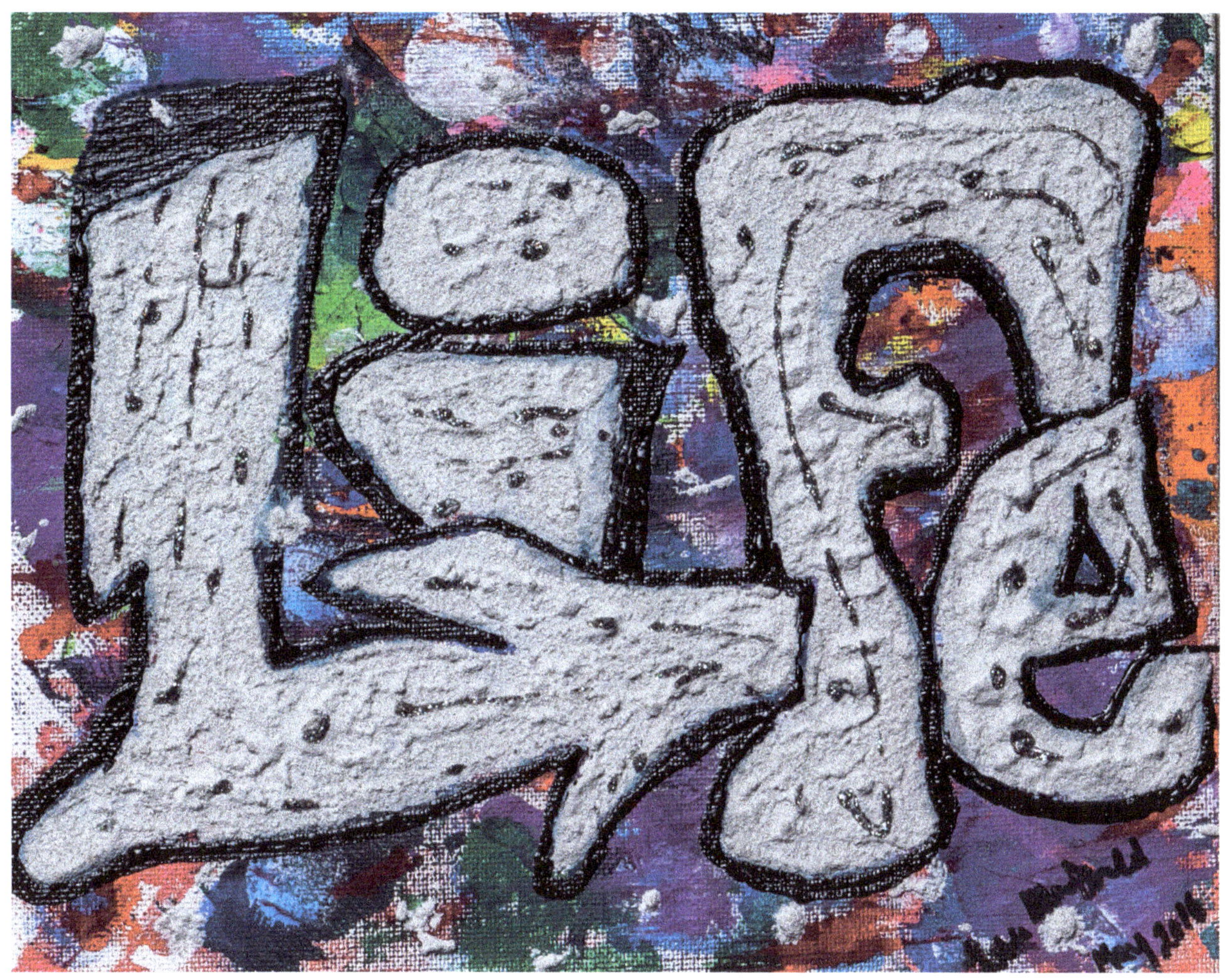

Life

May 2016

The word "life" is small, but profound.

When I was younger, my life was simpler, even blissful at times, dominated by my great family. As I got older, I experienced losses, such as friends leaving, family moving far away, and people I cared for having unexpected accidents and even deaths. It was hard for me to see these terrible events in a positive way.

As I've grown up, my perspective on life has changed. Life isn't easy. I learned that the hard way by dealing with anxiety. As I struggled, I used to think, *I'm the happiest girl there is. How could I ever feel this way?* As I matured, I began to think, *Life is teaching me to be strong—no matter what obstacles I face.* I showed life that I am not weak and that I won't let my anxiety get in the way of my dreams.

In this painting, I drew the graffiti word "life," and I used sand and paint to create the roughness and bumpiness, symbolizing life's ups and downs. I added glitter to indicate the learning gained from mistakes or learning experiences. The colors in the background reflect the happy moments I've had with my family and friends that I will hold in my heart forever. Those happy memories ease my life because whenever I'm down I think about the good times. This helps me continue my journey and live life how it should be.

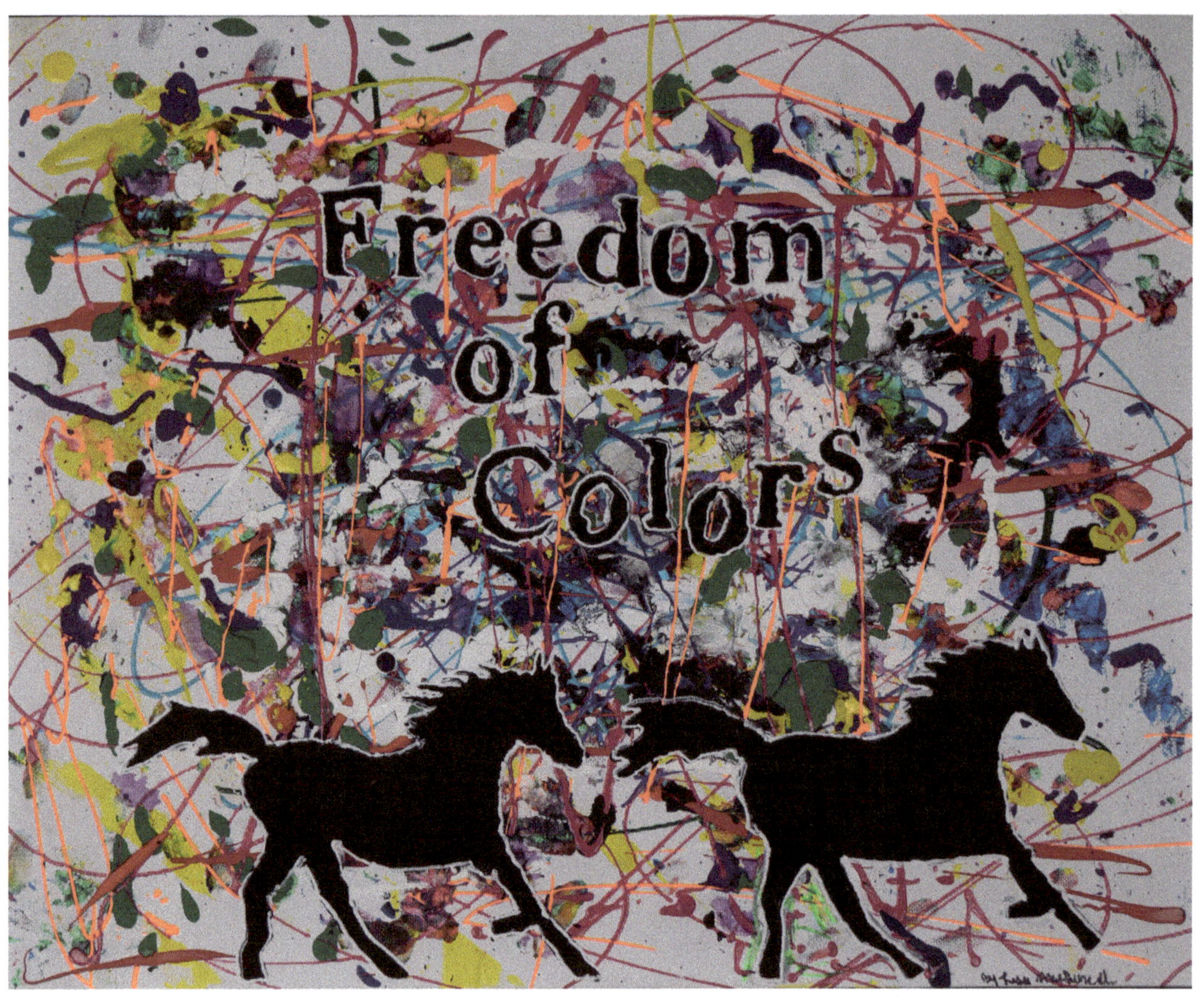

Freedom of Colors

2012

I created this painting about the life-changing event when Zane Landis came into my life at a most difficult time. I view our relationship as a work of art, full of happiness and love. I give him my heart and soul—just like I do with my artwork.

Zane has shown me how to let go of all my negativity and start living life freely. He helped me to find who I am and understand that being myself makes me so unique and loveable. He lends me his hand and leads me into a positive path. From the moment we met, I knew in my heart I wanted to marry him.

We worked on this painting together to describe how I feel about our relationship. Zane and I splattered the acrylic paint onto the canvas to symbolize our crazy times together. In fact, we had fun spattering the paint onto each other too.

The phrase "Freedom of Colors" expresses how Zane gave me the freedom to show my true colors and not be ashamed of who I am.

Finally, the best part of this painting is the two horses running. I chose horses because I always loved them, and they symbolize freedom to me. Zane is the first horse, and I am the second horse, symbolizing the impact he has made in my life by showing me that it is okay to be myself.

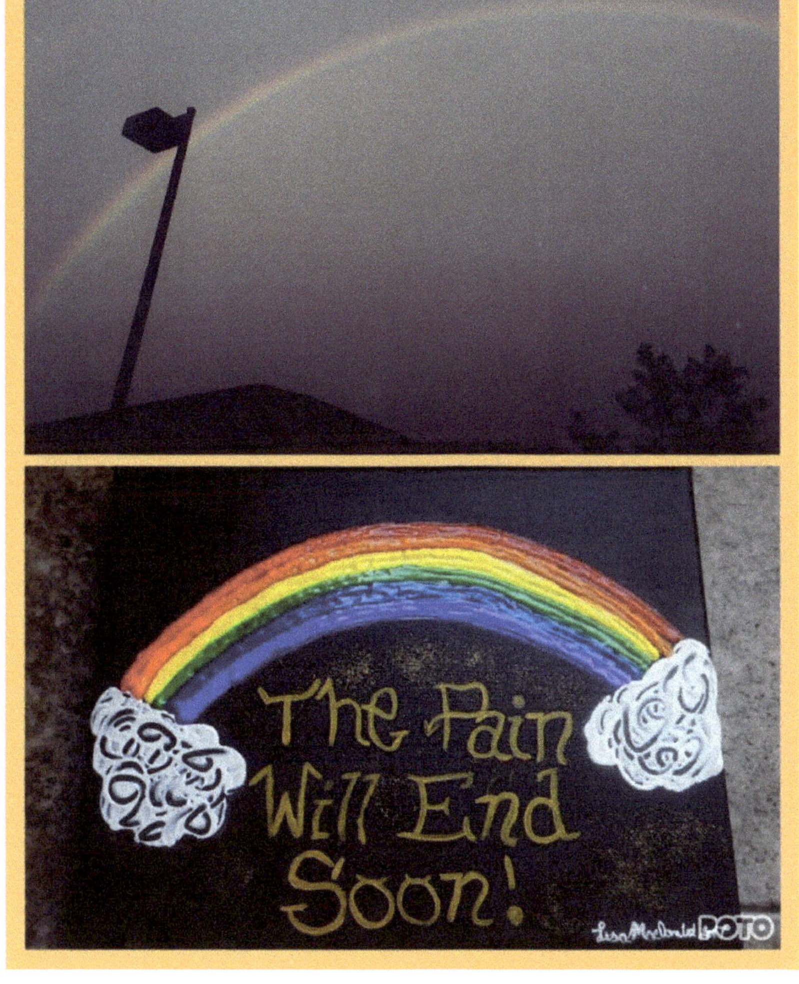

The Pain Will End Soon!

September 2017

I made this positive painting for myself when I was recovering from wisdom teeth surgery. Life can be mentally and physically painful, and sometimes it's hard to see what's on the other side of our pain. When we are in physical pain, it can be difficult to understand that the pain will end soon.

When I was in pain from my wisdom teeth surgery, it was hard to imagine feeling better. I could only focus on, *This is like a real nightmare*. I could barely sleep or eat, and my mouth tasted so nasty. I was not patient with the pain. In fact, I was in a mental breakdown.

By the second week after my surgery, I started to feel a little better. Everything went well at my follow-up visit, and I was ready to go back to work. The next morning, as I went out to get into my car to go to work, I saw the most beautiful rainbow I had ever seen. I thought, *That is a sign. I feel that I should acknowledge this moment.*

That rainbow helped me understand that we need to have thunderstorms and rain to allow a rainbow to shine through. We might deal with pain for quite a while, but if you make it through the pain little by little each day and take care of yourself, soon the rainbow will shine through for you.

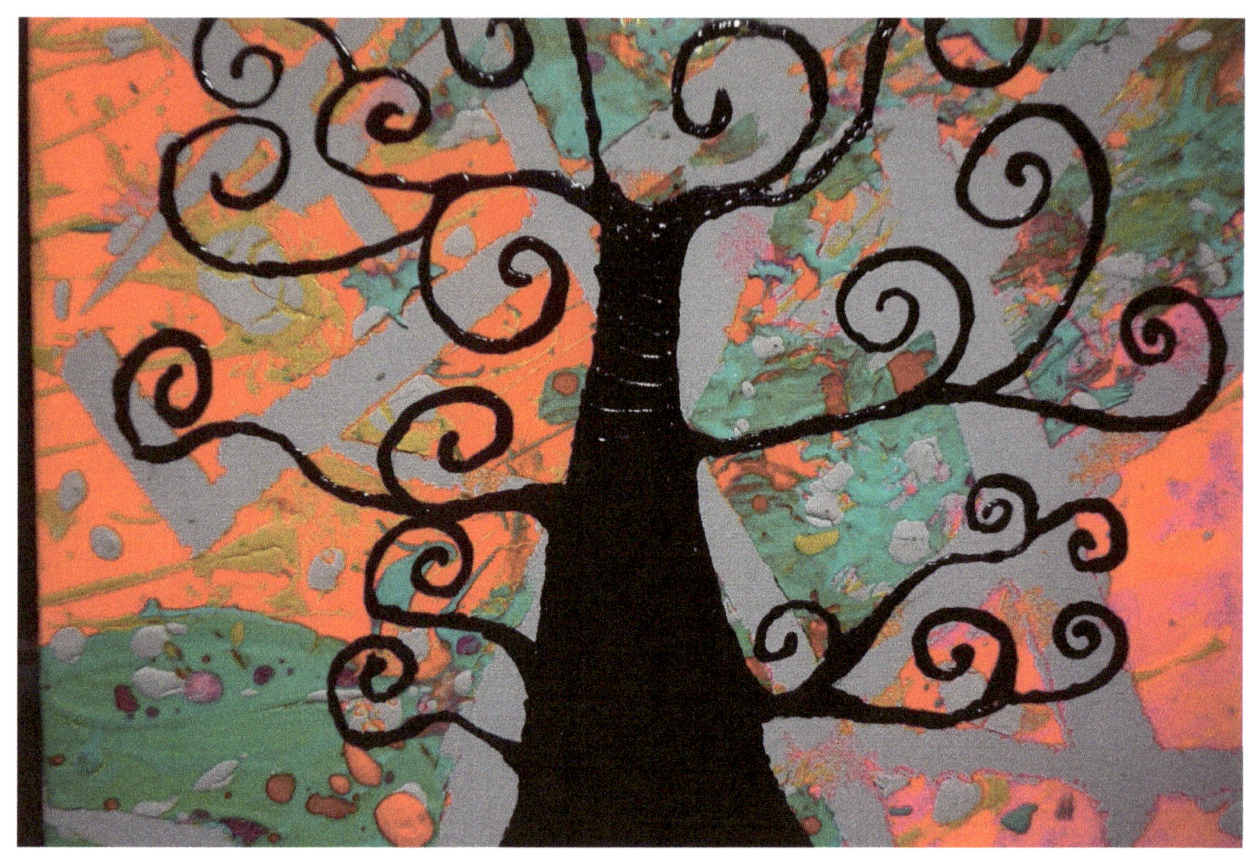

Poise Tree
June 2013

Splatter paint, rip tape, and squeeze puffy paint: Those are all things I've done to let my anger out. The day I painted this piece, I was so angry that I didn't think this piece would turn out nicely. I was painting anything that came out of my mind, when suddenly I took a step back to look at it and thought, *Wow, I released my anger into a piece that is beautifully vibrant.*

I made the background lines with tape, and hearing and feeling the tape rip helped me to release my anger. That made me feel good inside. Next, I splattered on the background paint, which was a great way for me to release the pressure I was feeling. I just let it go. Today, looking at my vibrant colors made me smile so purely and warmed my heart.

I decided to make the tree dark—but beautiful—because I believe that everyone has a dark side inside of them. I used black puffy paint for the tree because at that moment, I was listening to hard rock music, which made me want to create a tense look. But it also makes the tree cute by creating the curls at the end of the branches.

I titled this work "Poise" to describe the tree's grace and elegance.

I am a happier, stronger person because I am able to release my anger by doing art. Looking back on this piece reminds me that no matter how I feel, I can make a masterpiece.

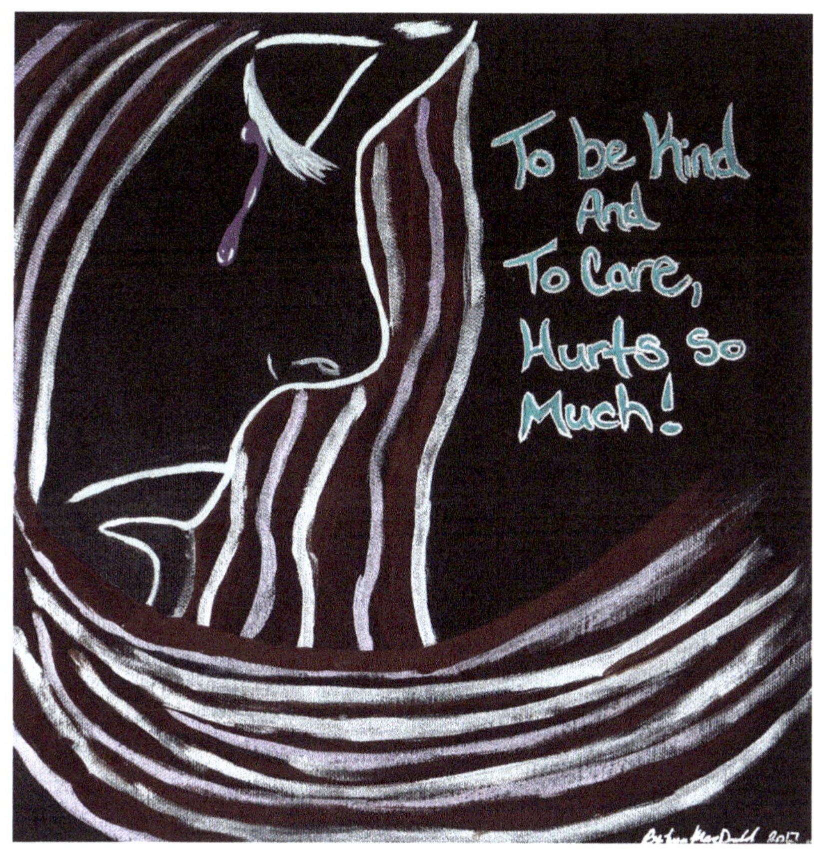

To Be Kind and to Care Hurts so Much! Struggle with the Past

2017

As I grow up, I have learned the hard way that people can take advantage of you and your kindness. For example, in my senior year of high school in 2014, I was bullied by girls who I thought were my best friends. Suddenly, they started hating me and calling me names. I was lost in guilt and confusion because I thought I had given them all my caring and kindness. That experience caused me to lose trust and to lose hope. Their words blocked my positive view of life.

I went downhill, experiencing anxiety and then depression, followed by lack of sleep and appetite. I felt that life was ending for me and that I shouldn't exist anymore.

Medication didn't help me, so I focused on counseling. My counselor sitting in front of me, listening to every bit I could express, really helped. My boyfriend, Zane, helped me a lot too, picking up all my missing happy pieces and building me up again.

A year later, I started to feel like myself again; however, at times I remember all those negative words, especially at night. Night was the hardest time for me to overcome my anxiety. I would cry and cuddle up with my cat and stuffed toys, feeling the intense loneliness in my room, feeling that the darkness was creeping up my head and scaring me with the past.

As days pass to months and months pass to years, I've been regaining my mental strength, my physical health, and my happy spirit. It feels great, whole, and full of life again. I feel that I can take on anything now because of how much I've gone through. Today, I think of negative events as learning experiences that made me stronger than I was before. Finally, I learned that what makes me weak can make me stronger. I know for a fact that I am a *strong*, independent woman.

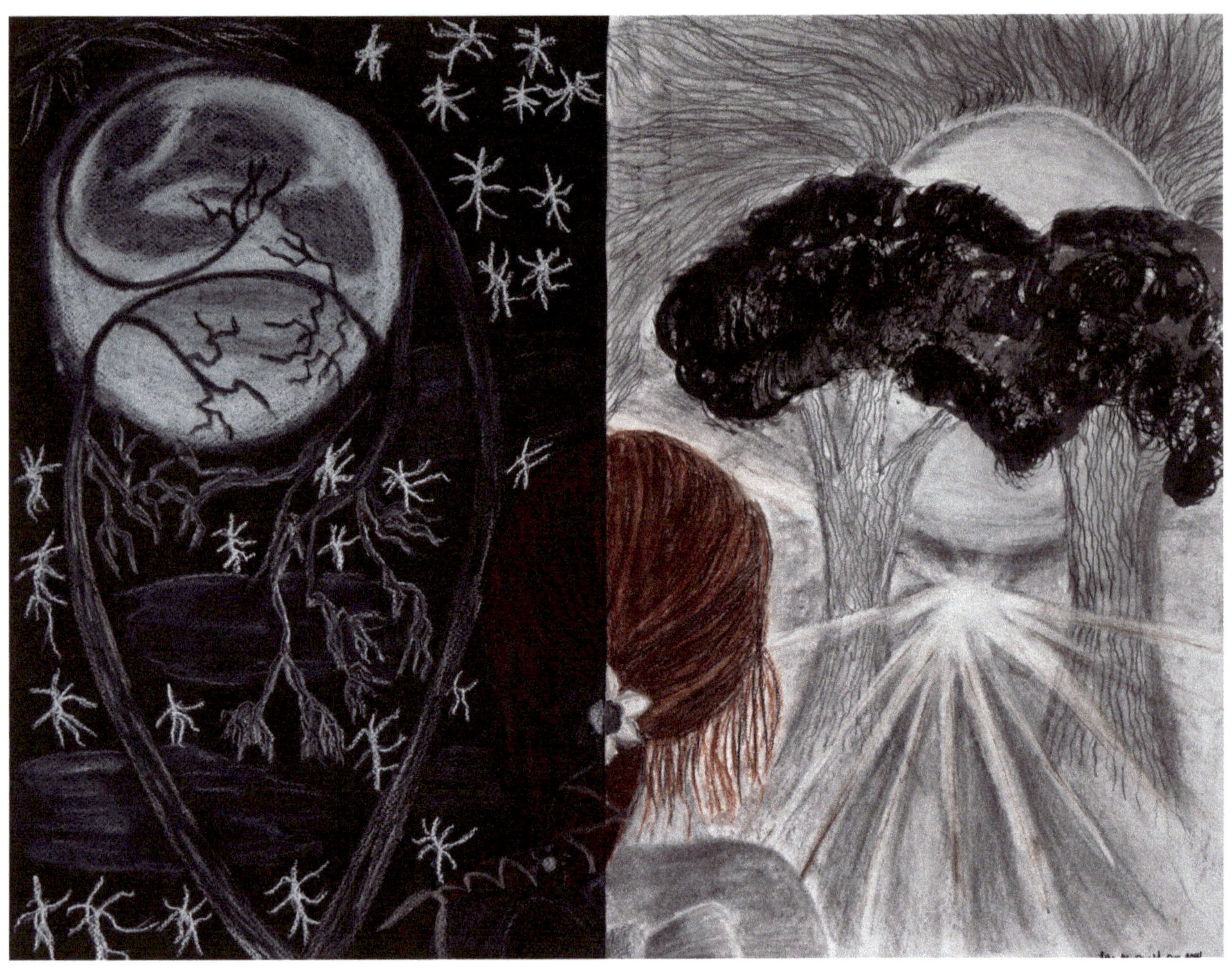

My Vision of Night and Day

2015

This piece represents my vision of night and day. I have always had difficulty coping with the dark and cold of the night. I see night as spooky, when tree branches create creepy forms that make me feel like I am in a scary movie. Sometimes I see the stars as bright as the moon, but other times they look as creepy to me as the tree branches. I feel lost in the dark, unable to see anything. I don't like being unable to see where I am going. The darkness reminds me of an endless, dark hole. An infinity of sorrow.

I love the day because it brings out the best of me, my true spirit within. During the day, I see all of the colors in nature. The sun's positive light and warmth energize my soul. When it's beautiful outside, I want to go spend quality time with the sun, air, and plants.

I have always wanted to travel to places that are bright and full of colors, to discover new things that the Earth provides. I also want to ride my bike or hike to places where I can engage with nature and learn about flowers and wild animals. I want to feel the cool breeze against my face and my hair flow through the wind.

As I see so much positivity during the day, I am practicing to also see the beauty and calm during the night. I am teaching myself to accept the night and to soothe my overthinking through meditation.

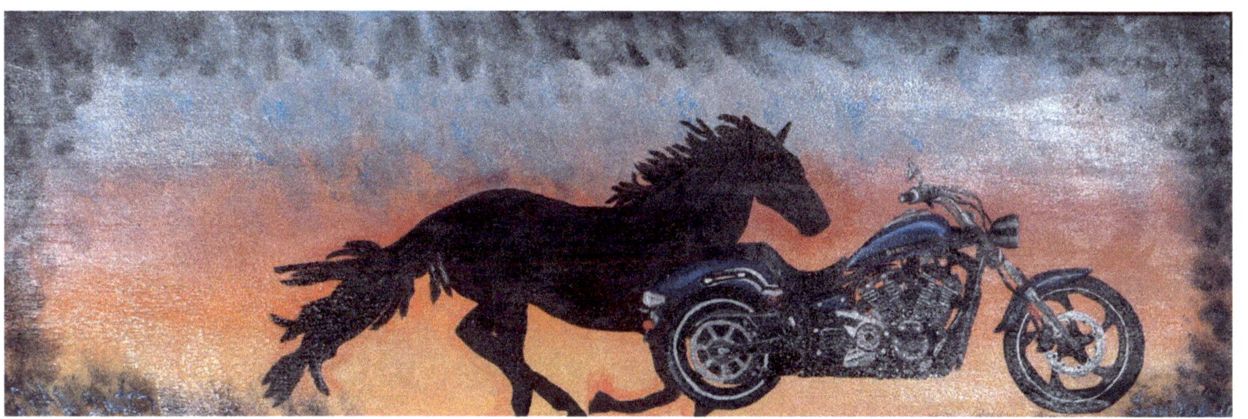

Motorcycle Freedom

2023

On bright, sunny, summer days, my dad loves to ride his 2014 Yamaha motorcycle. I know how special his motorcycle makes him feel, especially riding it.

I've been riding with my dad since I was little girl. I enjoy doing it with him. I love to feel the wind blowing through my hair and rushing through my helmet.

I always love when my dad finds nice country roads through beautiful Pennsylvania valleys. We'll often pull over to the side of the road and take a break to really embrace the view, to embrace the beauty and peacefulness of nature all around us. To me, it's paradise, something I would want to embrace every day of my life.

Today, as an adult, I don't have the chance to ride with my dad as much as I want because I am busy figuring out what I want to do in my life and working on my career. I miss it, and I am grateful for my childhood memories. I know soon, I will get back on that motorcycle and embrace it even more than ever!

I decided to paint this painting because I wanted to capture what riding on my dad's motorcycle feels like. When he drives fast, I feel like I am riding a wild horse on an adventure to freedom. When I am on the motorcycle, I envision myself riding bareback on a mustang horse on these country roads. That gives me so much happiness in my heart and soul.

Riding with my dad gives me the chance to relive my childhood life and feel free. I leave the worries of being an adult in this complex world behind me, and I'm in this moment with my dad.

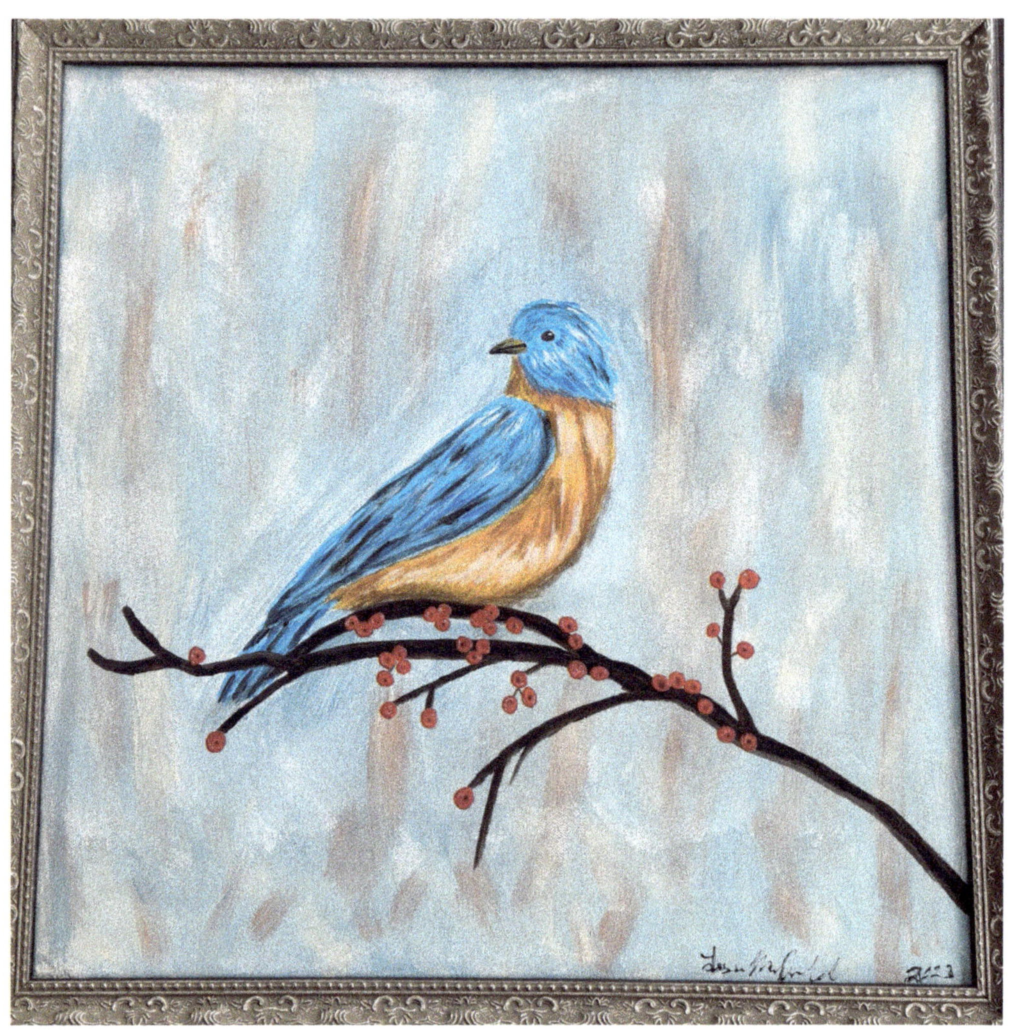

My Mom As a Bird

2023

My mom has always adored birds. Every morning, she sits in the kitchen, drinking her coffee and watching the birds out the window. I see that it gives her comfort and love because it gives her a sense of the freedom that those birds have. To me, birds symbolize independence and freedom, qualities I admire in my mother.

My mother is a very hard-working woman who will do anything in her power to make sure her kids have a great life. She grew up in Dominican Republic in a poor country area, without a lot of things. When she moved to the United States, speaking little English, she learned that by working hard, she will receive the things she needs.

My mother is a fighter, yet she is not afraid to ask for help when she needs it. She goes where she needs to go to do what she needs to do. My mother is the most loving and humble woman you would ever meet. People adore my mother and love to be around her. Her friends know that they have someone special in their lives, who shouldn't ever be taken for granted.

I painted this piece for my mother because I believe that birds are her spirit animal. They fly free, and they go place to place to get the job done. Birds socialize with other birds and fly in a group. When birds have babies, they work hard to find food to feed them.

I painted the bird in blue and beige because those are my mom's favorite colors. It turns out the bird I painted resembles an actual bird called an eastern bluebird. I painted the bird in the front and center of the canvas to demonstrate that after all the hard work my mom has done for her family, she deserves to fly free, to go place to place, and to embrace herself and her life.

My mom is a true inspiration. I see her as my twin because I was born on her birthday, April 6th. We have similar mindsets, and we do the same things. We always speak about our crazy dreams, analyze their meanings, and discuss how fascinatingly they connect to our waking lives.

My mother is also an amazing listener. Whenever I have a hard time in life, she's there to listen. She gives her all to help my brothers and me to have the best lives that we could ever ask for because she didn't have what we have here in America. She wants us to smile and know that there is nothing here to worry about, that we are blessed and safe with her arms around us. When it is my mother's time to leave this Earth, I know that there will be a bird flying above me that looks like the bird in my painting.

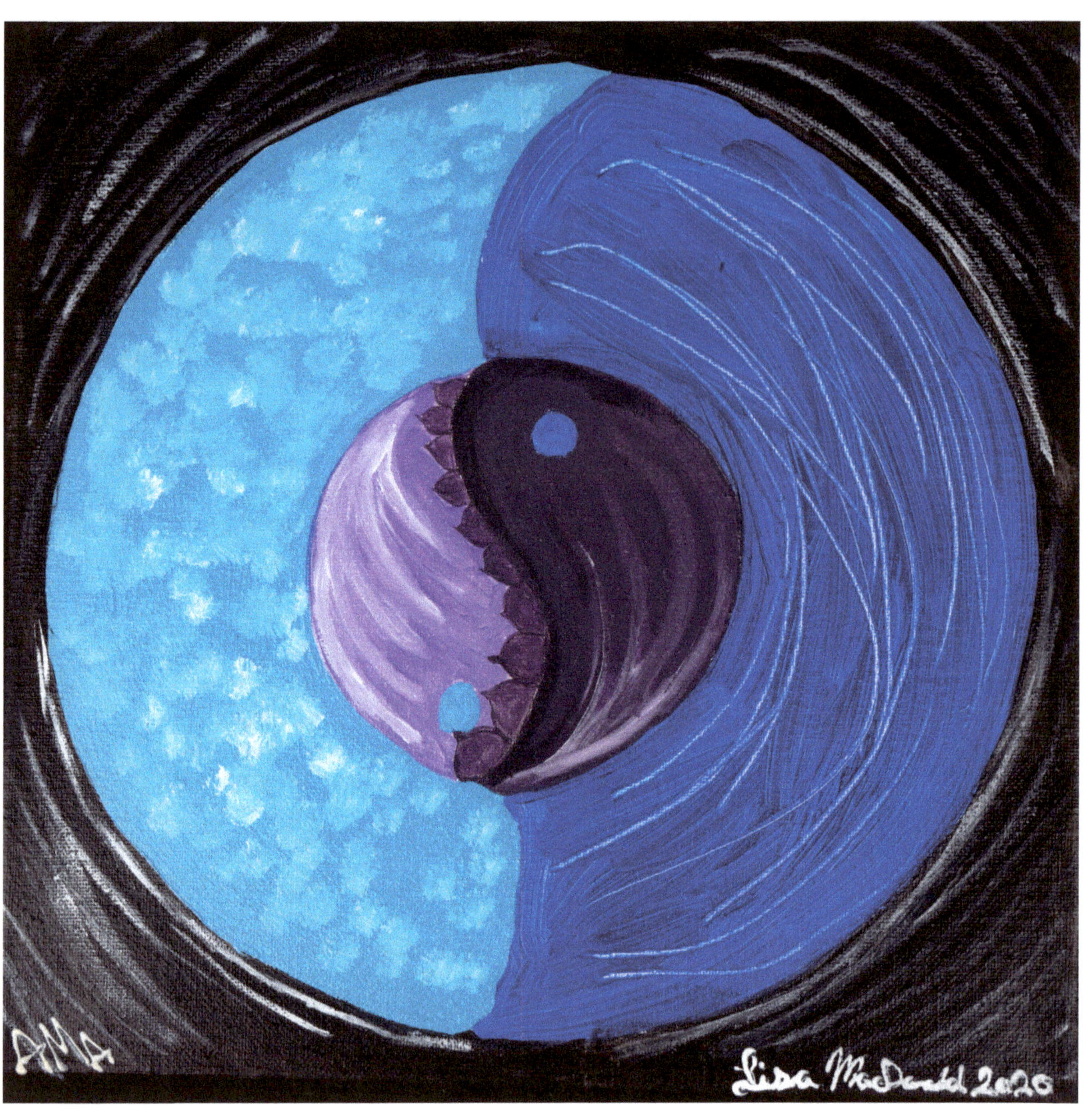

AMA
Lisa MacDonald 2020

My Life as a Ying-Yang

2020

Ying-Yang represents the importance of having the balance of negative and positive in one's life. Having too much positive or negative energy can imbalance your life and yourself. This imbalance of energy can make it difficult to face challenges. It is important to balance positive and negative to keep your focus and motivation.

This outer Ying-Yang in this painting represents my parents' personality traits. It shows how their different aspects molded me into the person that I am today. Then the inner Ying-Yang is reflected in my personality.

The light blue around the Ying-Yang represents my mother, who is so positive, passionate, and loving. Light blue is her favorite color, and it also resembles her softness and beauty. She's patient with me no matter how angry or sad I get. She is always there to listen when I need to let go of the negativity. My mom always has a positive mindset no matter how challenging life can be. She always has a smile on her face and is willing to help others. She works hard to provide a stable, loving life for me and gives what I need to live my dream.

The dark blue signifies my dad, who is very stern and hard-headed and doesn't like to take any excuses. The scratch marks evoke a feeling of how he is as a father. My dad has a strong mindset, and he is always pushing himself to succeed. He is a hard worker and thinks very logically at work. He was plant manager in a rendering factory and moved to working in a chicken factory. He is very intelligent with understanding the way people are and he is smart with numbers.

Outside of my father's hard-working job, he enjoys being outdoors, exploring nature, and especially running. He ran 115 marathons. He has a great sense of humor and cracks funny jokes. He can be silly when he embraces his inner childhood.

My parents' personalities created the balance that I needed in my life. The lavender resembles the warmth and love my mother gives to me. My mother created me to be a sweet young lady with an incredibly positive mindset! She taught me to be my own woman and to fight for what I believe in. She taught me to find my inner voice and speak it aloud through words and my artwork. She taught me the importance of providing others with positive energy.

The dark purple signifies the strength I have gained from my father, who created me to be strong-minded and to prove myself that I am worthy in this crazy world. He trained me to look at the world in a different way, to appreciate nature, and to learn to take the hard times now so that they will affect me less in the future. My father also taught me to always have my guard up and how to protect myself when dangers comes.

Observing my parents' different positive and negative balances helps me gain an understanding of the impermanence of life. It gives me an understanding that life is never going to stay the same and that I need to learn how to manage both the good and bad times. Observing my parents' personalities has made me a wiser woman.

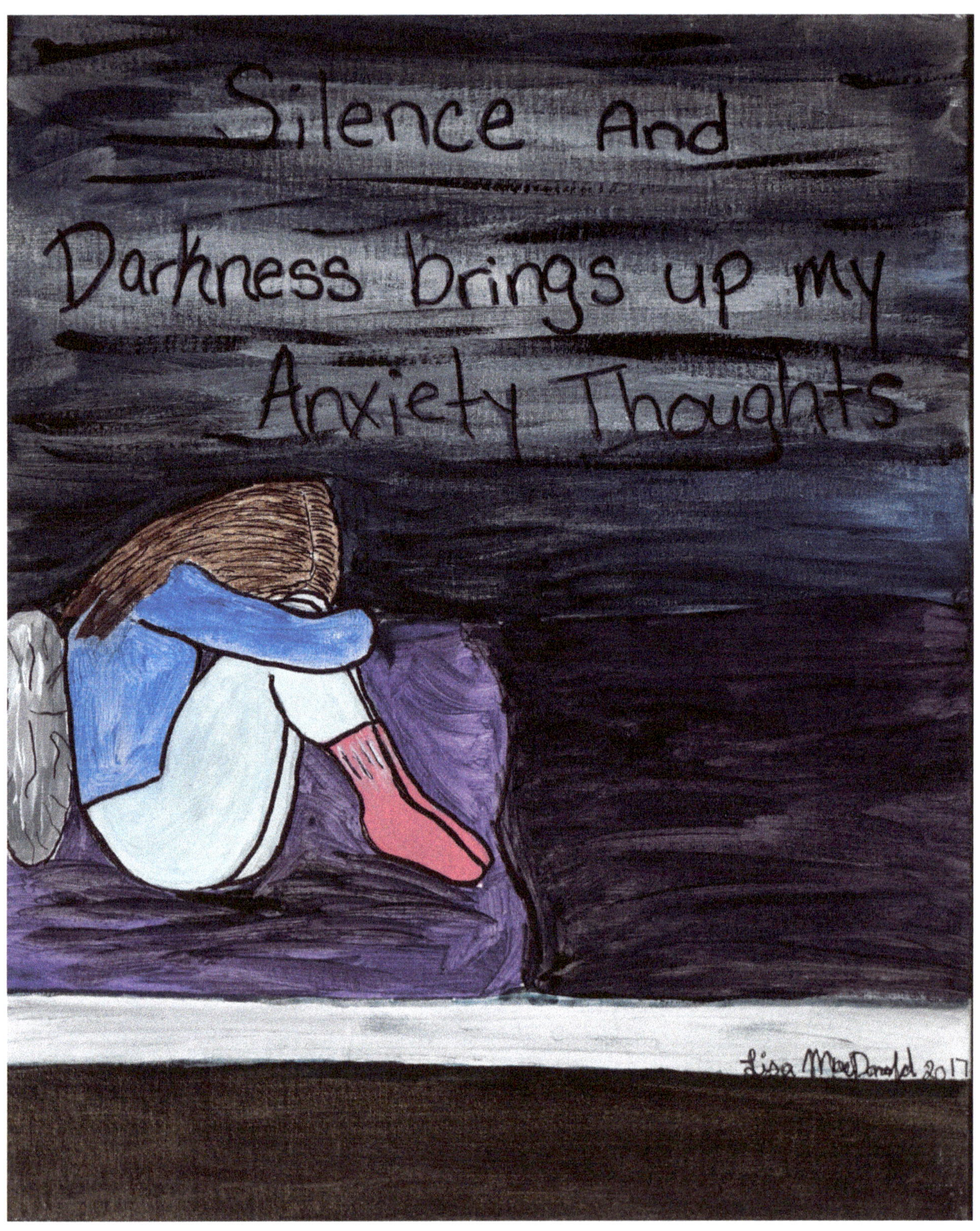

Silence And
Darkness brings up my
Anxiety Thoughts
Lisa MacDonald 2017

Silence and Darkness

2017

When it's time for bed, my thoughts used to haunt me and take me on a dark path. The negative energy inside me got me all worked up. It made me want to cry. The darkness covered all my artwork in my room, and it made my soul feel empty.

When I was alone in my dark room, I got flashbacks from when I was bullied and taken advantage of in high school. I also fought to accept that my brother wasn't home anymore because he was serving in the Marines. I felt hopeless, like I couldn't control my mind. All I saw is darkness.

I found it hard to sleep with all these crazy thoughts in my mind, trying to cope with all the troubles I had in my past. People saw me as a happy positive person in the daytime, but at night before I went to sleep, I shed tears when my negative thoughts took over my mind:

Am I enough for this world?

Am I capable to beat my battles?

In the morning, when I got out of bed and looked outside, the sun gave me the energy that I needed. I felt like I was living two sides of myself: One was positive me, and the other was negative me. Nights were always difficult for me, but no matter how negative my nights became, I always gained the positive light in my days.

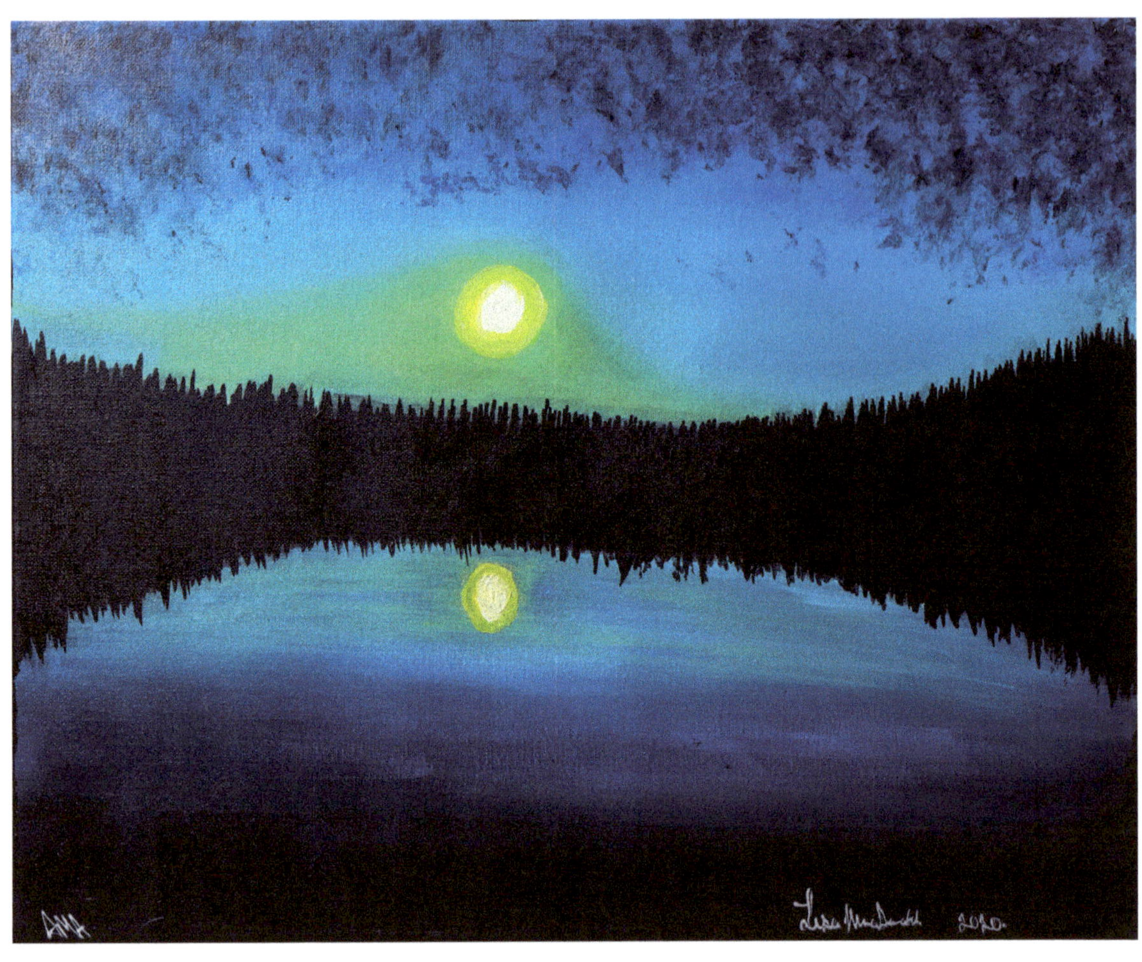

Moonlight Shadows

2020

Nighttime is scary to me. When it is time to go to bed, my mind starts racing. I think, *How will I get to sleep with so much noise in my head?*

When I created this painting, I had been training myself not to fear the darkness, but rather to see the beauty in it. By the time I completed this painting, I felt that the night sky has a quiet shining moon, which brings warmth and stillness into my whole body. It teaches me to stay within the moment and to take a break from the intense, high-energy day. I also sense how beautiful it is to be still and how nighttime teaches me to work with my mind and to relax myself.

Nighttime reminds me to slow down and reflect deeply on my day. I ask myself, *What did I accomplish today? What am I most proud of? What am I grateful for?* I smile, knowing that I am motivated and capable of making things happen in my life.

Looking at this painting brings peace into my dark night and lets me know that there is beauty in every night.

"I often think that the night is more alive and more richly colored than the day"—Vincent Van Gogh.

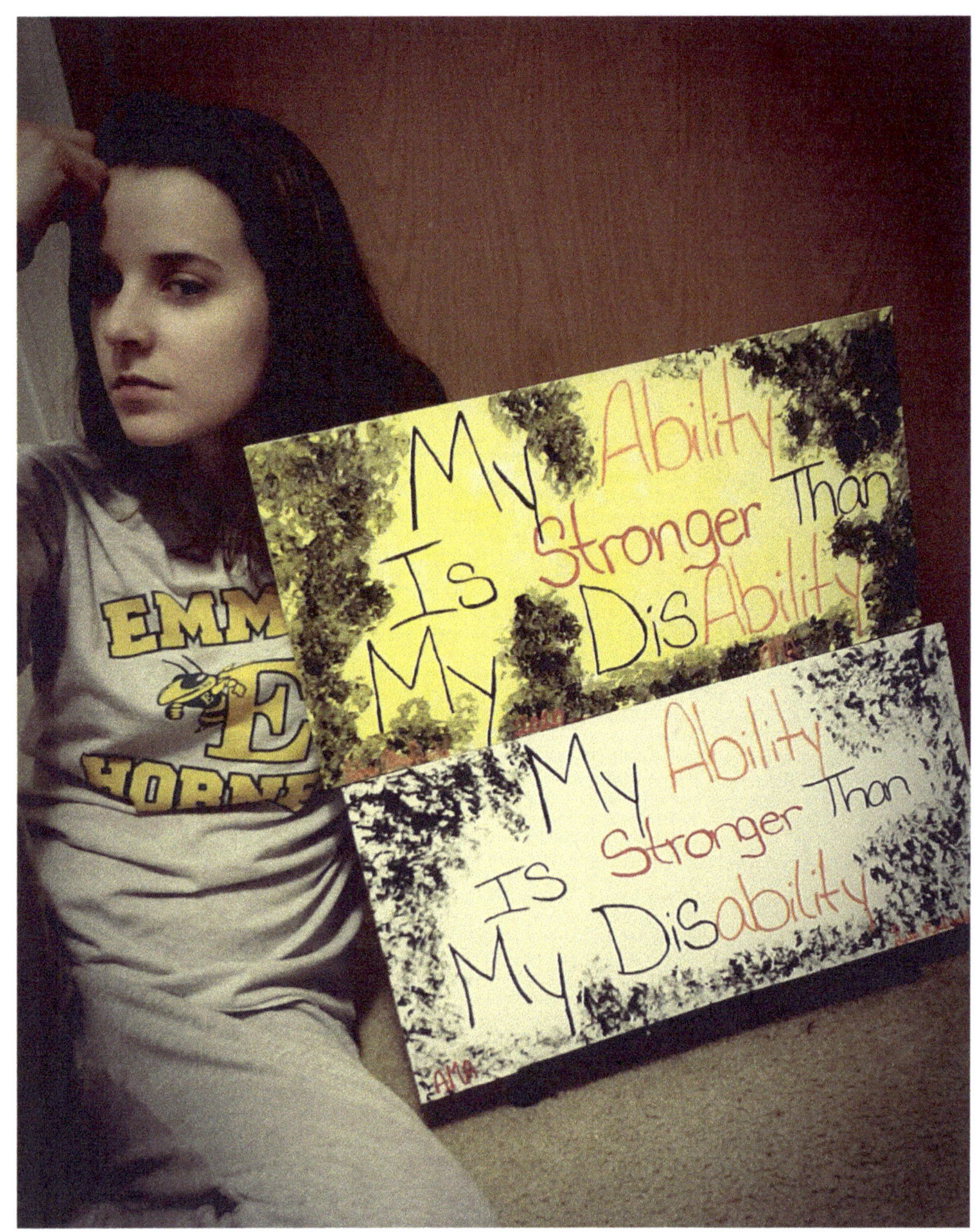
My Ability
Is Stronger Than
My DisAbility
My Ability
Is Stronger Than
My DisAbility

My Disability Quote to You

2020

During my twelve years of school, I struggled so much with my learning disability that I had to take English as a Second Language classes (ESL) and speech therapy.

I define learning disability as something that causes a person to struggle with a particular subject, so that it takes them longer to process and comprehend complex material.

I have always struggled with math, writing, and reading comprehension. When I was in kindergarten, I spoke Spanglish, and I mixed my vocabulary up so much that I had to repeat kindergarten. One time, another student said, "Speak English or go back to your country." In high school, students made fun of me and ignored my ideas because I sometimes messed up my words.

When I got to college, it felt like an answer to a prayer. Finally, I got the chance to express my ideas through clubs, hosted my first-ever workshop, and even had my paintings hung in Lehigh Carbon Community College, Cedar Crest College, and other public places. I finally felt like an artist, having achieved my childhood dreams.

I never let my disability get the best of me. I push myself to strive on. I will never give up on making my dreams come true.

As an adult, having worked on many different types of art and having done lots of mediation, I know a lot about myself and what I am capable of. Now I see my learning disability as a gift—rather than a curse. My disability gave me a different perspective on life than most people have. I appreciate the people around me. I don't judge other people, and I am very patient with others.

The reality is that everyone has some sort of a disability. Are you willing to make it your strength?

I have learned that we are simply human. We are made differently, by how we process things, how we do things, and how we live our lives. Instead of judging another person, listen to their story. Try to put yourself in their shoes. That will give you a totally different perspective on how different we are. We are all meant to work together and embrace everyone's differences and imperfections.

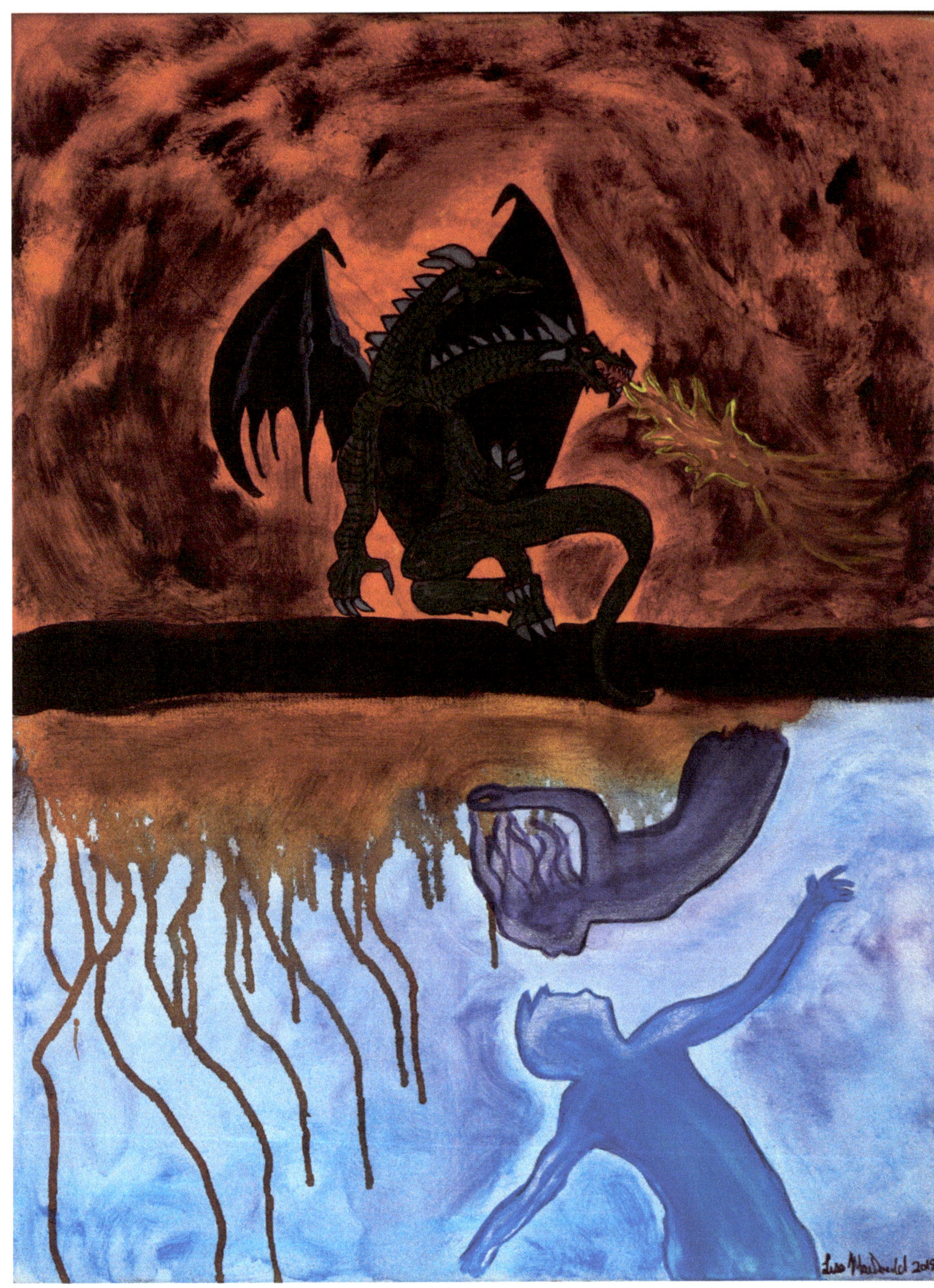

End-of-the-World Dream

2018

I created this painting to abstractly capture what happened in a dream, to bring my dream to life in a beautiful work of art.

One night, I dreamed that the world ended, and I was the only living person on Earth. The world was burning after being flamed by the two-headed dragons. In my dream, seeing what was going on here on Earth, I decided to drown myself in the ocean. Once I went down into the deep, dark ocean, I saw only darkness. I could feel myself losing my breath and wanting to die.

Suddenly, a figure of bright light came up to me, with his hands stretching toward my hands. I didn't know what to do, but held his hand. The man took me down deeper and deeper into the ocean.

Later, I felt like I could breathe, and I saw a magical, beautiful place down deep into the ocean. It was like another part of the world, filled with happiness and soothing colors. In my dream, I noticed the man who took me by my hands was my boyfriend, Zane.

My dream showed me that Zane had given me a whole new life to live and a whole new perspective on our world. The dream showed me that no matter how hard life can be, if we have each other, we can get through anything. We are built to be strong and keep this relationship going no matter what happens.

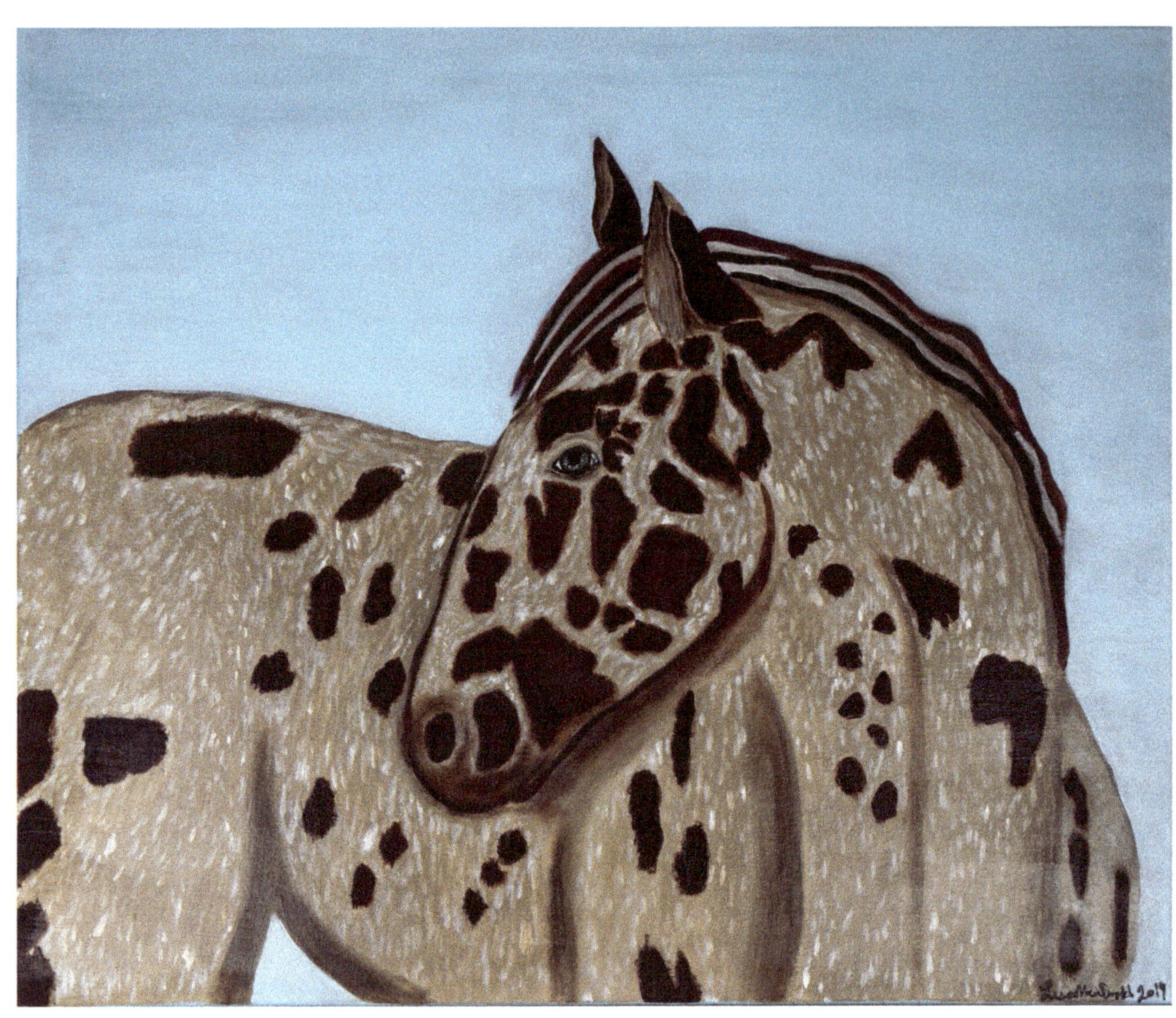

Me as an Appaloosa

2019

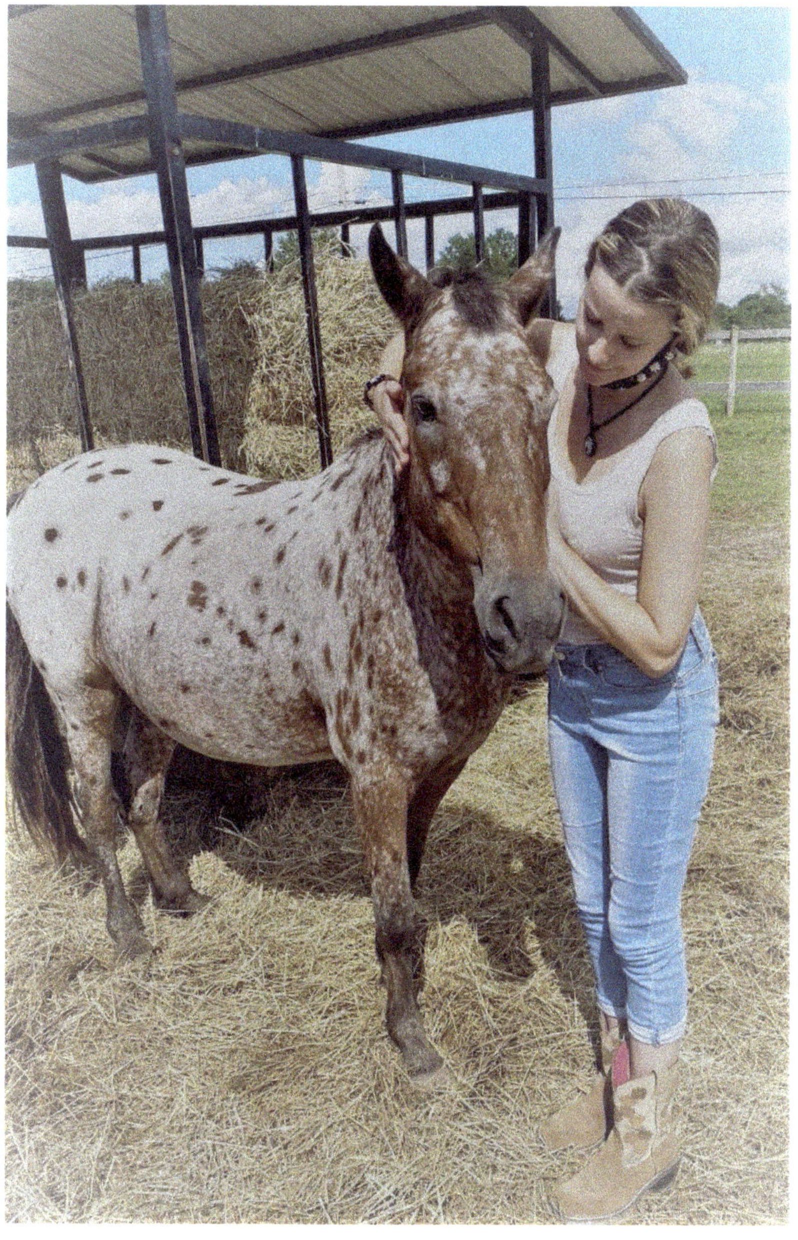

Since I was in sixth grade in 2008, I have always wanted to see myself as a horse. I have never seen myself as a typical girl; I would always have rather been a horse. I always wanted to feel free like a horse and run through beautiful lands of nature. I never felt like I belong in this human world. I decided I would be an Appaloosa because they are so imperfectly beautiful, covered in unique spots.

For this painting, I added brown for the spots and brown with highlights on the mane because it looks similar to my hair. I also gave the horse hazel green eyes like mine to really make it feel like me as that Appaloosa horse!

Seeing the finished product made me feel so emotional because I have been wanting to do this since 2008. Completing this painting motivated me to search for an Appaloosa horse. I found an Appaloosa pony in a barn in 2020 in Quakertown, Pennsylvania. This Appaloosa pony looked similar to my painting, and I was in tears when I got the chance to meet him. I couldn't ride him because he was a pony, but hugging and petting him made me feel like I envisioned I would way back in sixth grade. That pony gave me a lot of hope for my future and made me feel like I can do anything.

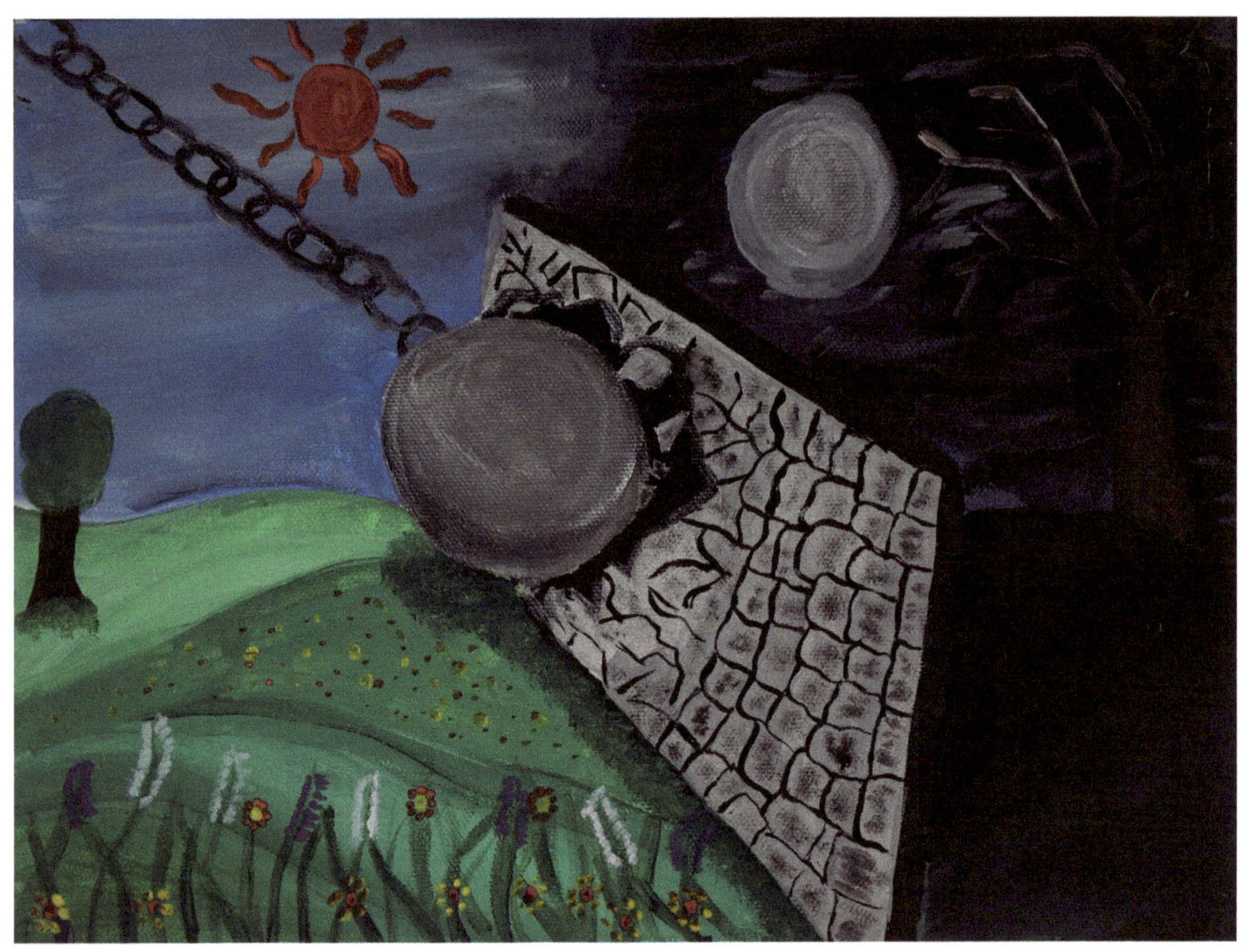

Struggle with the Past

2018

After getting bullied in high school, it still haunts me in my day-to-day life. I try to keep positive and do things that make me happy, but when I stop doing those things, my bad memories come back, grab ahold of the past, and throw it at my face. I take two steps forward, then four steps back.

I can be hard on myself, telling myself, *You need to move on from this. You cannot hold on to this for the rest of your life or it will be a waste of your lifetime.*

I decided to take the time to be my own therapist. I painted this piece to feel where I am at in my life. On the outside, my life seems great, and I seem to be heading in the right direction toward my future. I have a clear vision of what I want my future to be.

But I have such a hard time looking toward the future because I constantly think of the past. But when the past haunts me, I stop and stare at a wall or my phone. In this painting, the haunting past is represented by the wall between my present and my future.

I know I have to make a change, which is shown here as the wrecking ball, destroying my past mindset so I can move forward to my future.

This painting gives me a special reminder whenever I get into that past mindset thinking. It reminds me to be that wrecking ball, breaking through that past wall. I am forever grateful for this piece and how much it helps me to fully live my life.

My Cat Carmel

2019

Growing up, I always had cats and enjoyed their company. Cats are always so comforting, and they teach me a lot about life.

First, cats have taught me how to live life at an easy pace, filled with relaxation and positivity. Cats are great reminders to take a break and relax.

Of all the cats I had growing up, Carmel was unique. I always had black or black-and-white cats, never a color like Carmel. My brother William and I picked up Carmel back in 2008 at my mom's friend's neighbor. At first, we didn't know what to name him because we couldn't tell the gender. When we found out the gender, my dad decided to name him Carmel.

Carmel was such a humorous, special little kitty. He always wanted me to watch him eat and to make sure I ate as well. I didn't like cooking much, but when he meowed at me so loudly, I was forced to be in kitchen to feed him so I might as well make myself something to eat too. I loved to watch Carmel when he got into crazy moods and would run across the kitchen floor and dash through the hallway into my room. My room was always the room he went into. It was like he owned it. He always slept with me and always loved to be very close to me, which warmed my heart.

When William left to serve our country in 2012 and in 2014 when I was bullied, I suffered a lot from loneliness and depression. Carmel sensed it. He knew I wasn't myself. I had a terrible time falling to sleep, so Carmel slept right beside my head and purred to help me relax. My doctor prescribed me medication to help with anxiety and depression, but it made me feel worse. Carmel noticed

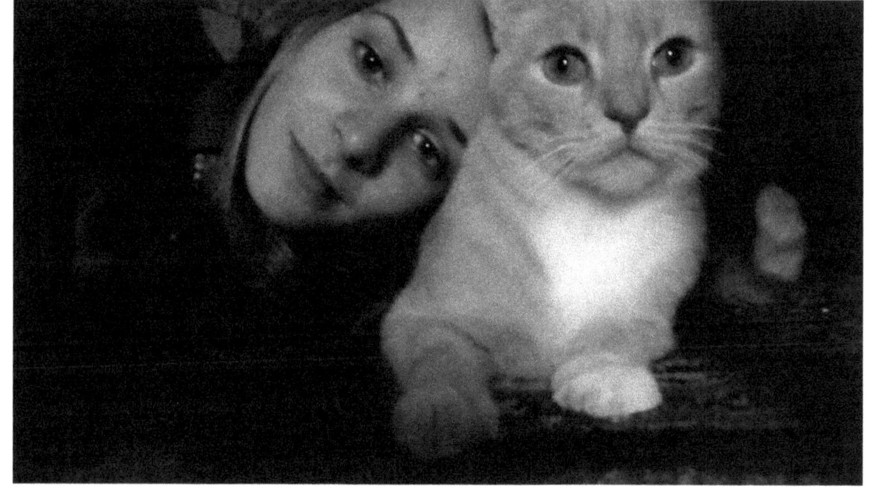

it so much that he was right beside everywhere I went, as if he was telling me to not give up on myself. He was such a smart cat, who could understand the negative energy I had going on in my life. He helped me through the nights, and he gave me the light in the days.

As years passed and Carmel grew older, I noticed so many problems with him. It terrified me. I didn't know what to do to help him. He had a flea allergic reaction, then came food allergies. It just kept getting worse and worse each day. After many trips to several veterinarians, we learned that he had a pancreatic infection. But still he got sicker and sicker. Every day, was a new challenge for him and for me, but I could not give up on him because he never gave up on me.

In 2019, I saw signs that Carmel wanted to go. He sat on my lap a couple of times and purred a lot. He was telling me that it was time for him to be at peace. I didn't want to let him go, but deep down I knew it was right for him to go.

April 22, 2019 was the day I decided to put him down to sleep and be up in heaven. Nobody wanted to go with me to the cat clinic, so I put my chin up, looked up at the sky, and took Carmel with me into the car. I couldn't hold back the tears. I just let everything go and held Carmel's paw as I drove to the cat clinic. When we got there, the receptionist took us to a quiet room and told me the steps they would be doing for him.

The moment of Carmel's passing was traumatic for me because I never knew how to handle death, especially right in front of my eyes. It was crazy for me to be in a room where one second Carmel was alive, and the next, he died right in my arms. I was devastated to know that my baby was gone forever.

This painting of Carmel was the hardest painting I have done both because mentally and physically. I had started painting it a couple months before he died, and I promised myself that I would complete it before the end of 2019. I pushed myself working through every detail of this painting. A lot of the times the fur didn't look how I wanted it to.

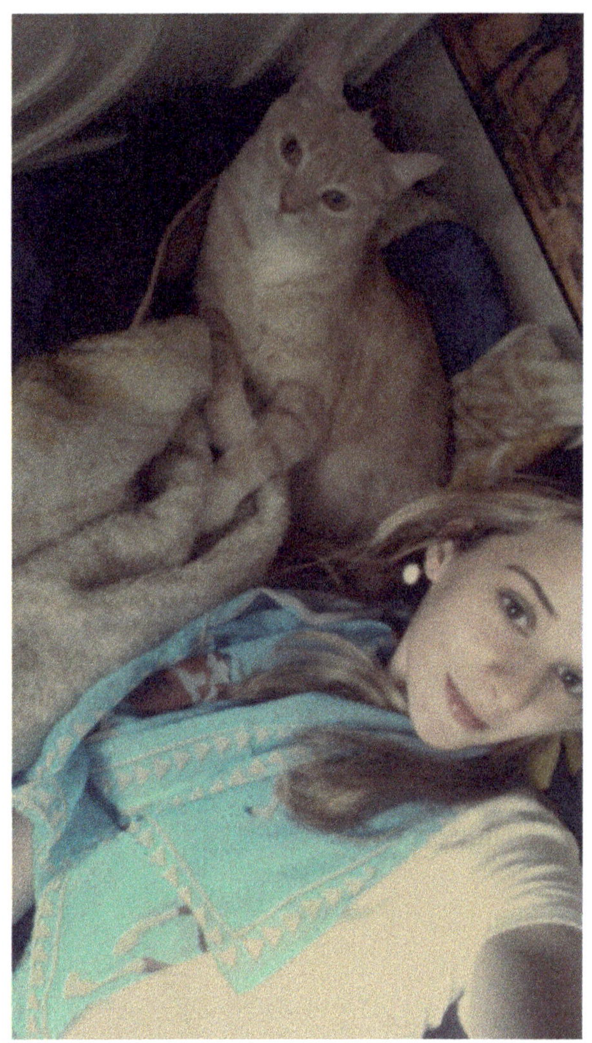

However, I began to notice that it was supposed to be like that because the cat was imperfect and he was going through such a hard time. I wanted to embrace his imperfections that he had after the battles he had fought in his life. He was still a beautiful, charming cat.

When the painting was complete, I felt relieved, knowing Carmel is alright. He will always be in my heart. I had this painted framed beautifully because Carmel taught me a lot about life. He taught me that I have to be at my strongest when I am feeling at my weakest. Even when he was in pain, he was still purring and rubbing against me as if it didn't bother him. Every day, I look up at this painting that's hanging in my room, I am reminded to be at my strongest when feeling my weakest.

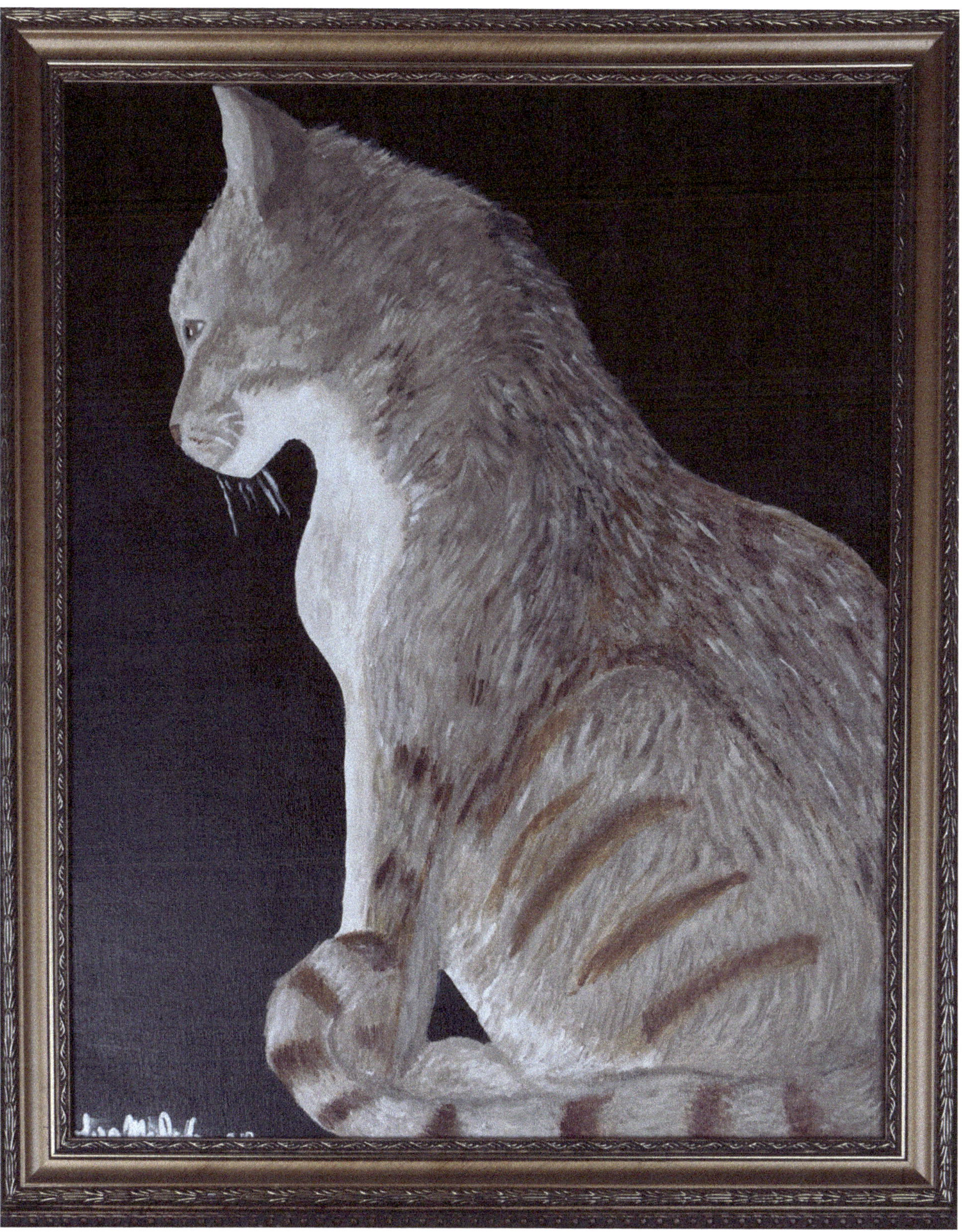

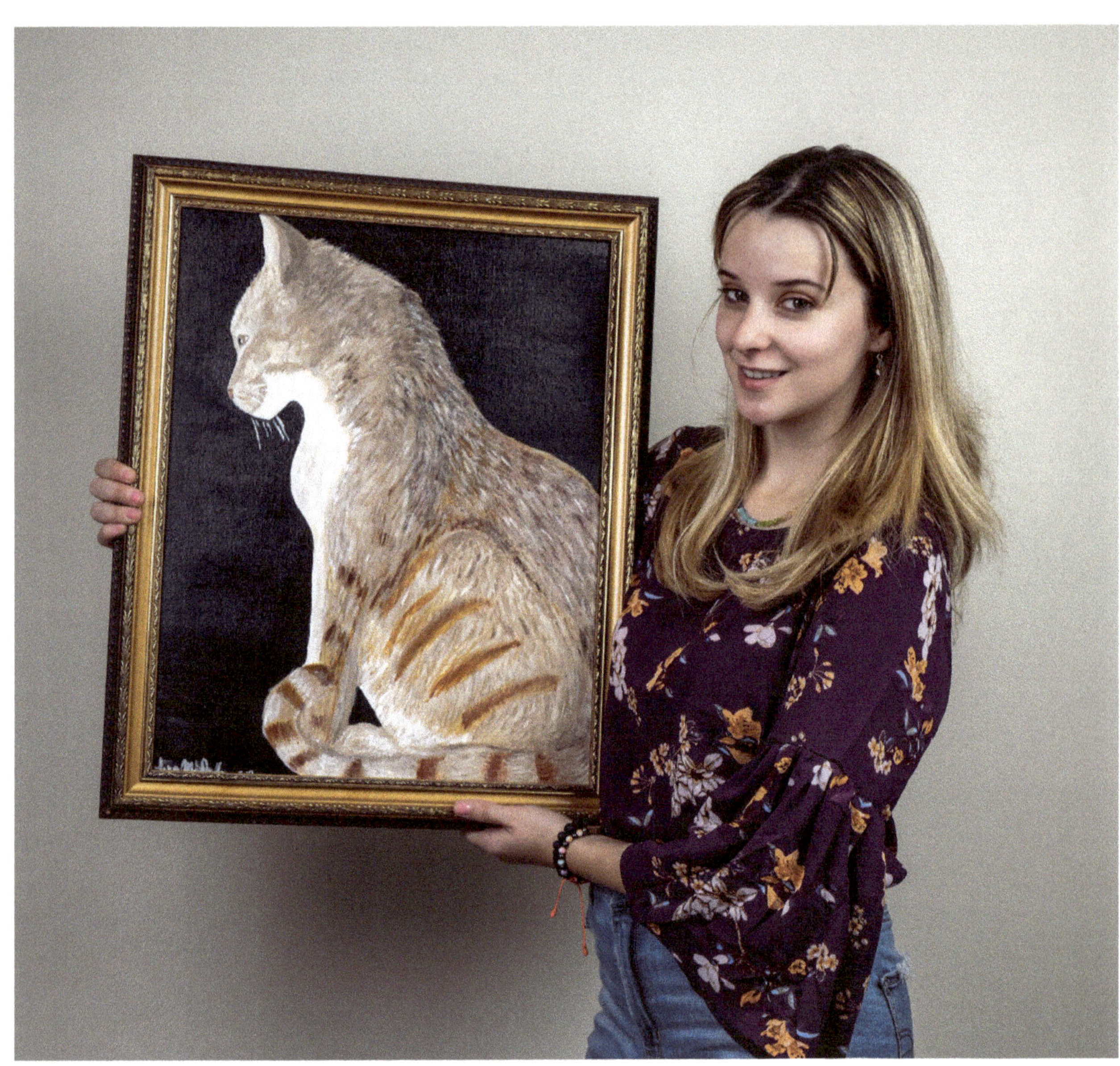

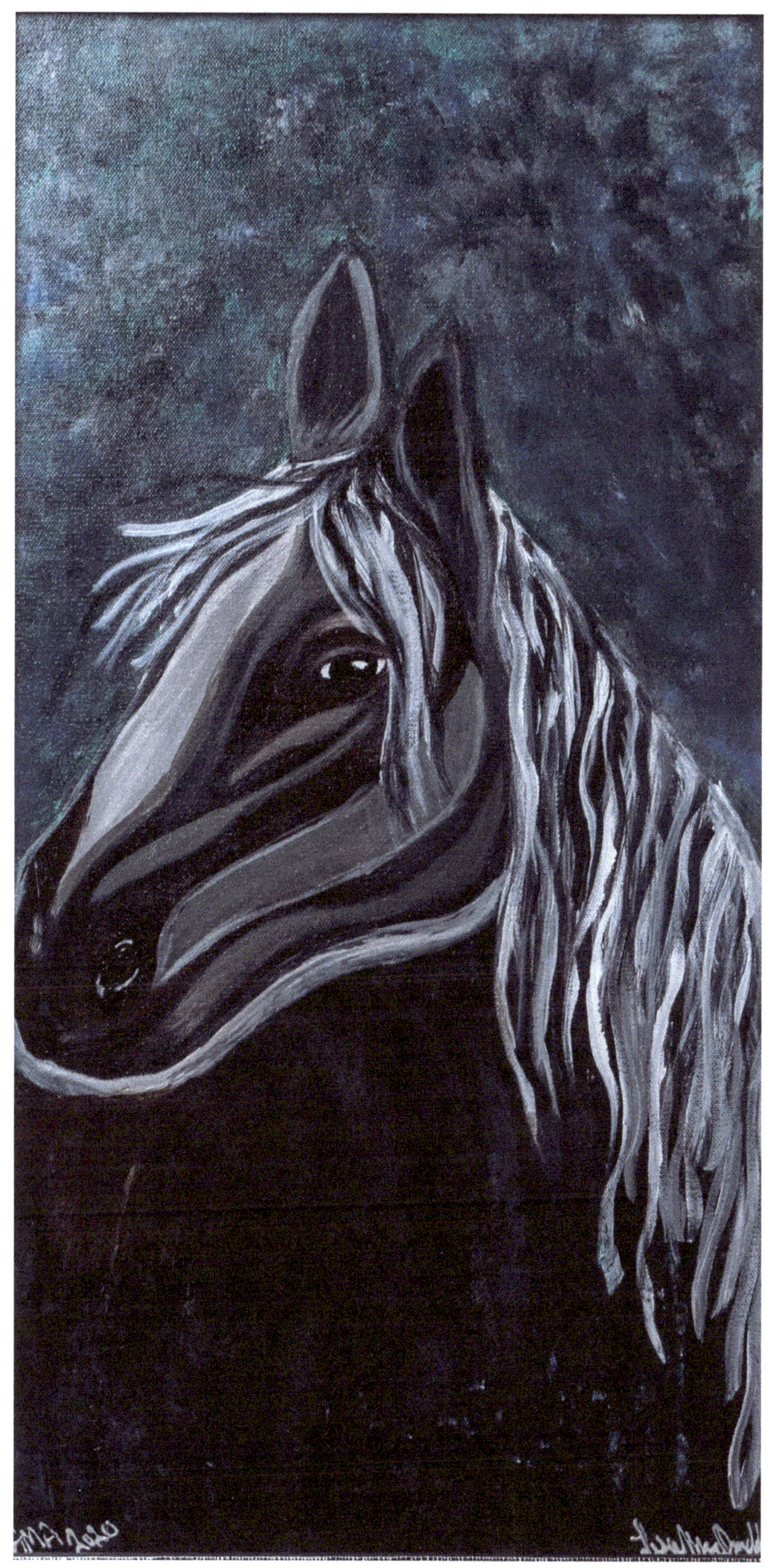

Warrior Horse

Summer 2020

I believe this is one of the most powerful paintings I have created. I knew I wanted to paint a horse, but I didn't know how I wanted it to turn out. I decided to go with the flow in the process of painting.

I listened to my gut feelings a lot because doing so helps me remain true to what I really want. While painting, I moved away creating a typical, realistic horse to a more fantasy-like horse. I like the abstract look of this horse, which appears like it could pop right out of this painting and become a real-life horse.

While I was working through this painting, I was also working through complications in my personal life. I noticed that this horse painting was getting darker and darker, and I added interesting elements to it. I added gray around the horse's face and made the mane black and gray with white highlights. I also added white around the face because I thought the mane and the outline of the face made the horse pop and glow from the darkness.

When the painting was completed, I stepped back to see how it looked. I sensed right away the strength of this painting. I felt that the gray around the face looked like metal and represented protection—like armor. Also, I painted scars that turn into the metal to symbolize how I have beaten my toughest battles and now I am stronger, wiser, and better able to beat any new life challenges that come in my way.

I named this painting *Warrior Horse* because when I look at this horse, I feel like I am a warrior, that I can be strong, and that I am an independent woman. When I have a bad day, I look at this painting and feel calmer. This painting reminds me to be strong and that the storm will end soon if I keep my head up, my mind straight, and my focus forward.

I decided to do a photoshoot with me looking like a warrior beside this painting as well, done at the Steel Stacks in Bethlehem. I wanted to show the world that Yes! 2020 is a crazy year with the Covid-19 pandemic, but I am here to be a warrior, to take a stand, and to be mentally and physically strong.

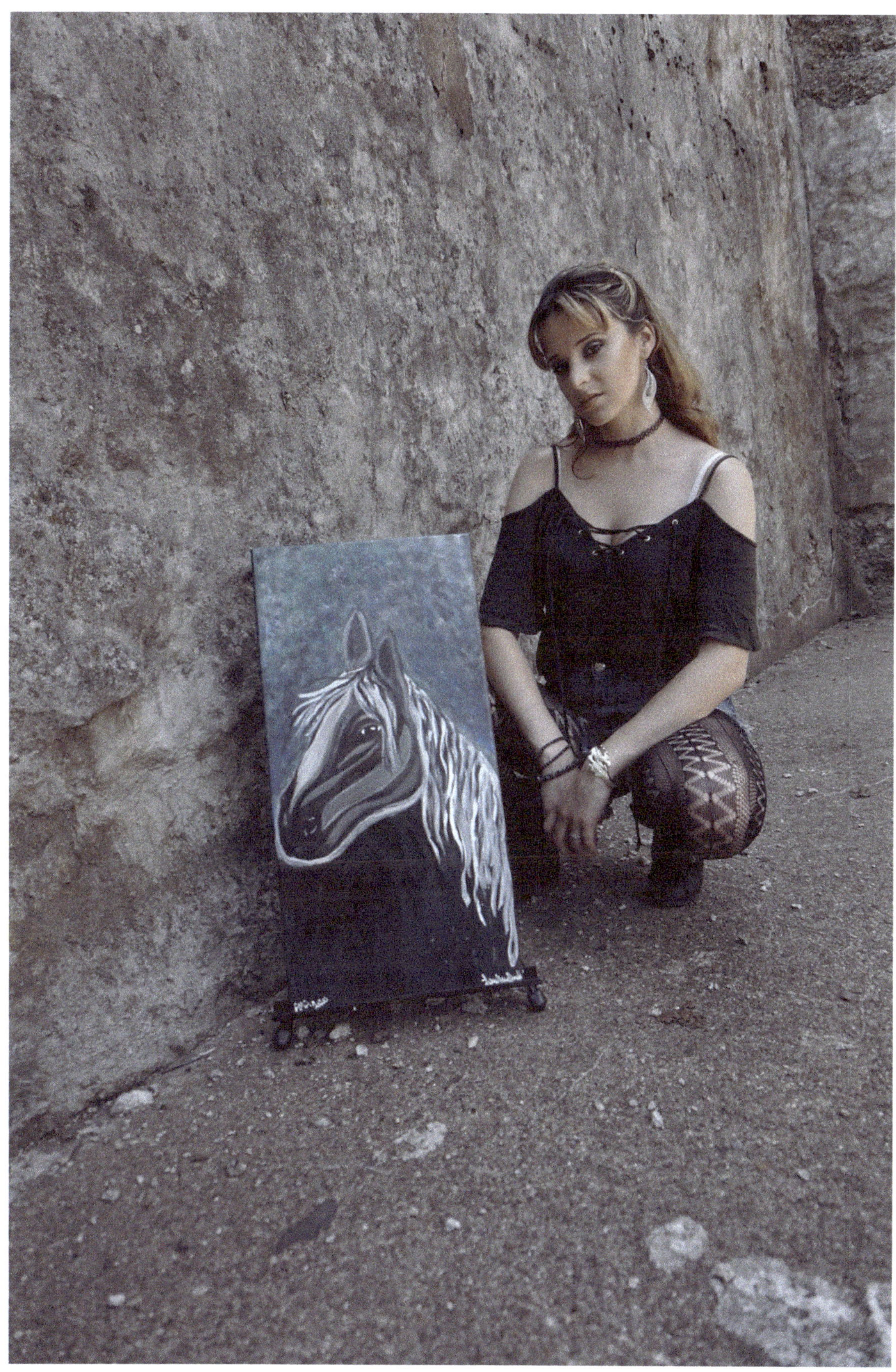

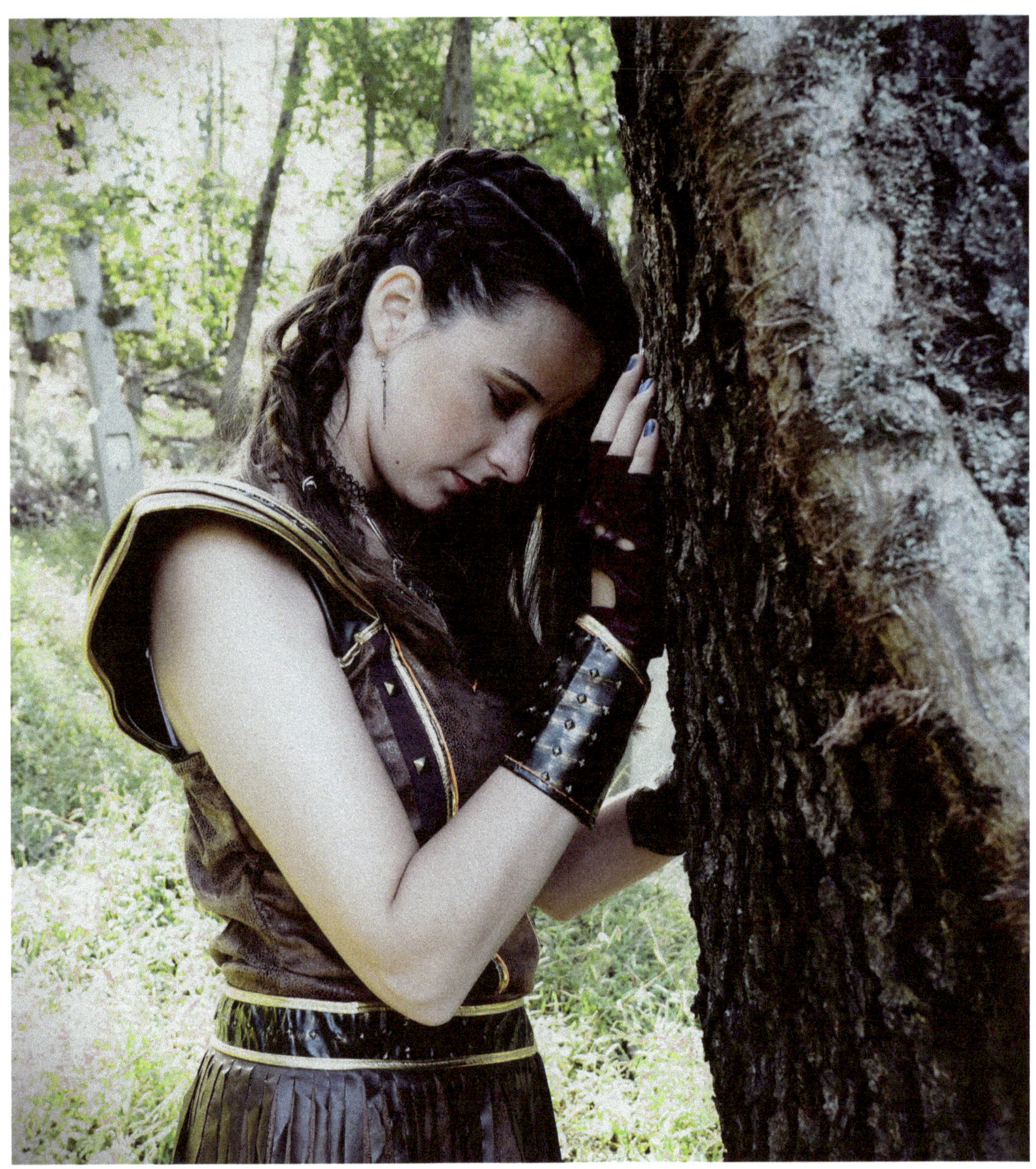

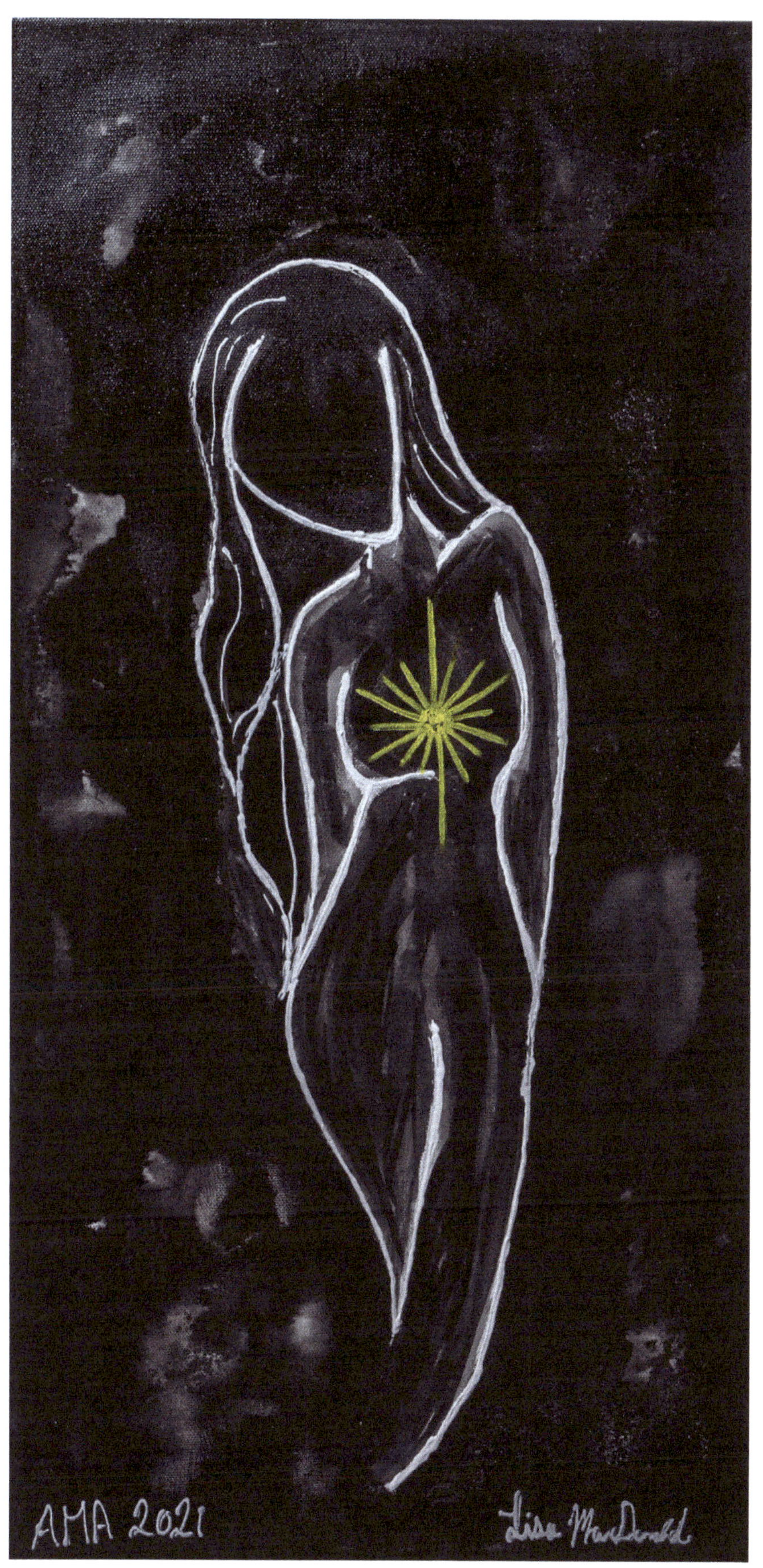
AMA 2021
Lisa MacDonald

Hidden Happiness

2021

Hiding your happiness is like having a mini version of you inside, screaming to come out and shine!

When I was growing up, it was hard for me to express my happiness. I felt that I had to hide my true feelings, especially in school. When I got home, I felt free to be me and express what I wanted. I enjoy spending my time with my neighbors Lester and Jo Ann because with them I can express myself easily without any judgements. In general, I am more comfortable being around adults because they care more and appreciate me for being myself. Sometimes I feel like I should have been born during a different era!

I know now that I shouldn't try to hide my crazy, happy energy. When I let my light shine from within, I feel relieved. I embody the true spirit of a happy person. This makes me feel like I can be who I was meant to be—no matter what other people think.

Today, in college I am able to be more like myself. I can shine onto other people and make them feel better about themselves. We all have an inner light. We need to let it shine and lighten up the world. As an Abstract Motivational Artist, I want to help lift other people up. I want to help them let their inner light shine. And let them know it is okay to be yourself.

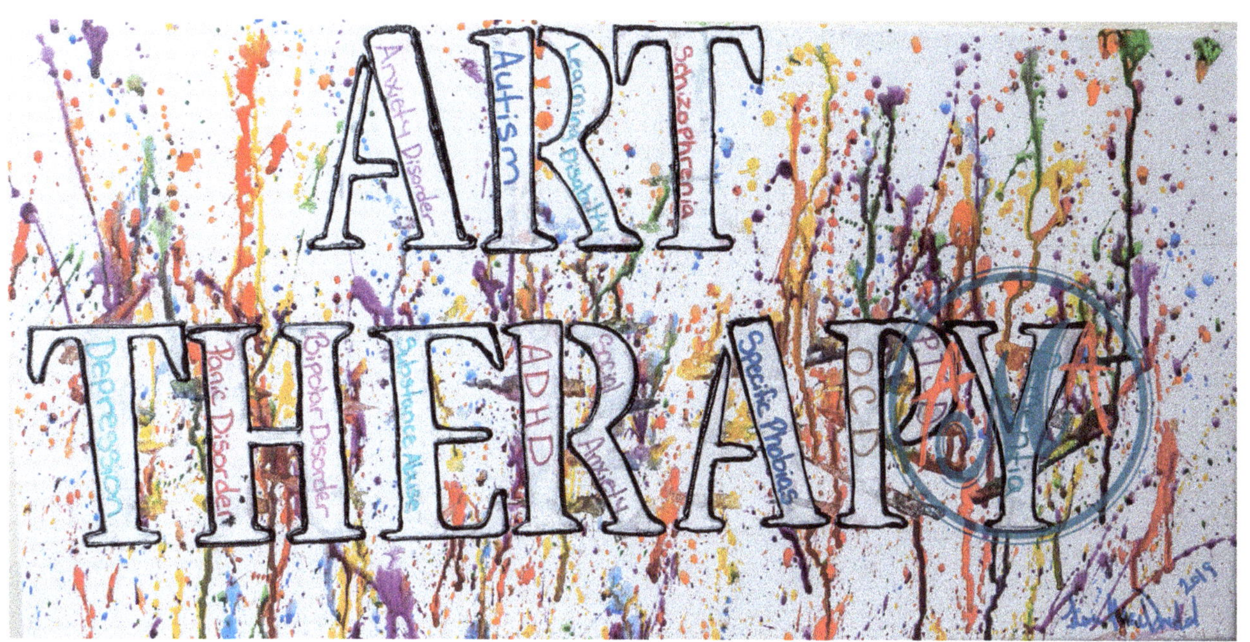

Benefits of Art Therapy

2019

If there wasn't art in this world, we would be losing our minds, living in a boring world. Art, music, and dance bring life to our minds and souls. We all need this to live life freely and to gain motivation when life hits us hard.

Art heals me because it allows me to express all my negative emotions onto a painting. It gives me a sense of accomplishments, and it teaches me how to understand what's been holding me back for years. Out of my whole life I have realized that the degree I am going for is what I have been doing since I was a little girl. I never ever thought to connect psychology and art together. I thought art was just a hobby and fun thing to do but realistically what I have been doing is what's been helping me to work within. No wonder I became such a high-vibrating person so full of imagination. Art really made me realize who I am truly and how for me to act like others isn't making me happy.

Turns out, all along I was doing art therapy. During hard times, art helped get me out of the negative feelings and reinstate the positive in my life. This motivates me to have others listen to my story and how I overcome challenges in my life. I feel like I taught myself art therapy and that I really gained the true knowledge what art therapy can do for others. As for myself who struggles with writing, words were super hard for me to express how I feel within. I believe art is so beautiful to use in a therapeutic field because it can help a person express imperfectly through any form of art because our emotions are imperfect and we should embrace the beauty of letting go through art.

With this painting, I wanted to capture the benefits art therapy offers. I included many mental health terms to express the variety of illnesses.

Many people of my generation have a hard time looking within themselves because they are so concentrated on what's on their screens. Sometimes when I talk to people, I can tell they have no control over themselves and their minds. For them, art therapy would be impactful to help them gain self-awareness.

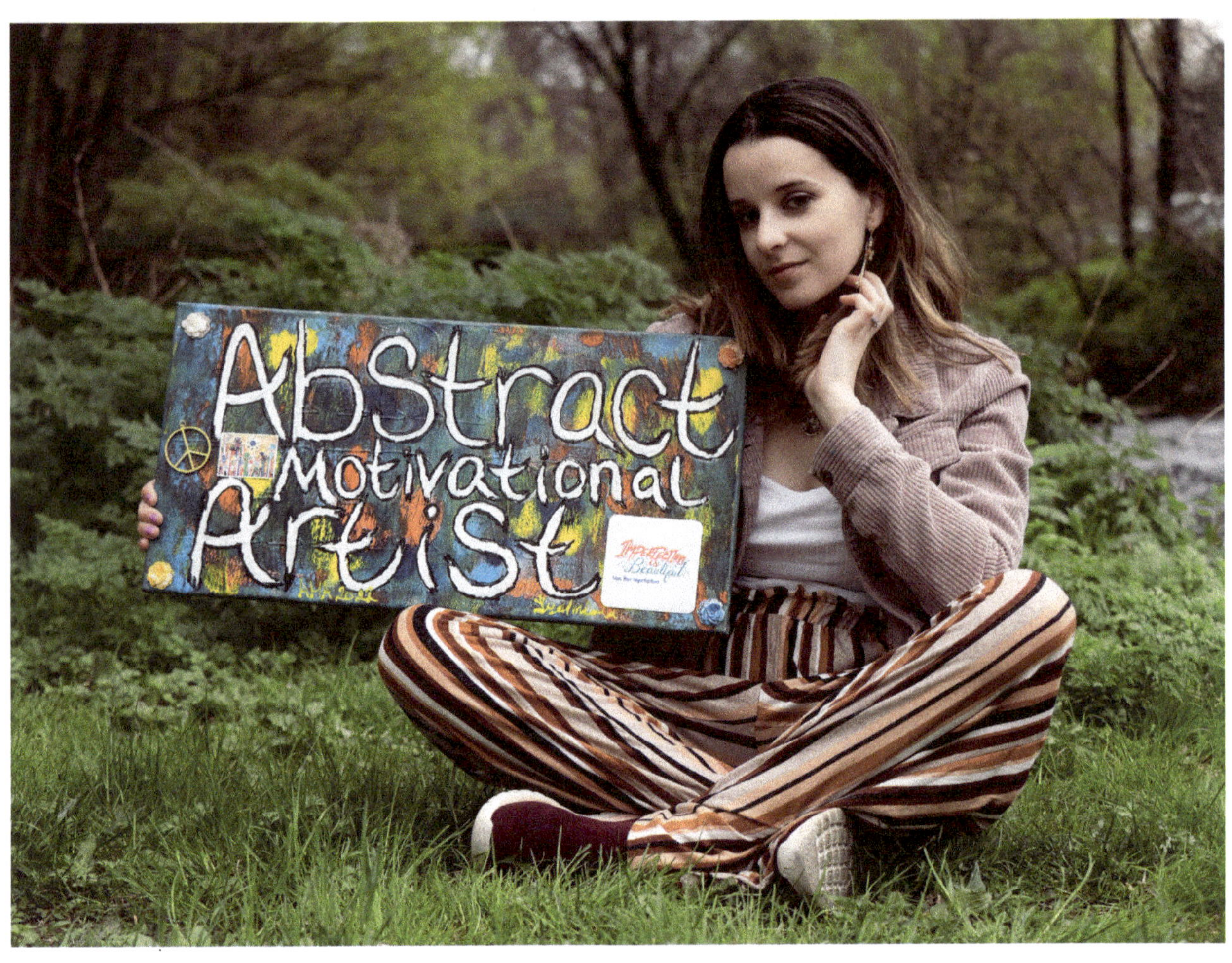
Abstract
Motivational
Artist
Imperfection is Beautiful

Abstract Motivational Artist

2021

In college, I thought I knew what I wanted to do in my life. I got a bachelor's degree in the arts at Cedar Crest College, but I found I was learning more in my work as an Abstract Motivational Artist.

Then I began a program to get my master's degree in art therapy, but started to feel very depressed, unmotivated, and burned out. I was conflicted between pursuing my master's degree and focusing on my Imperfection Is Beautiful business. After a lot of soul-searching, I decided to drop out of college and focus 100 percent on my business.

After making that decision, I felt happier, more confident, and freer than I had in a long time—perhaps since I was a little girl. Finally, I feel like I have control on where I want to go in my life. I don't have to worry about due dates. I work at my own pace, and I strive to be happy where I am at. I decided to paint over Art Therapy painting and include Abstract Motivational Artist. I added my business colors and different elements that represent my business.

Since I have taken this path, many people have told me I have inspired them and that they see how I can make an impact through my art. I was even offered a job to help people with mental illnesses. That made me realize how much my art can make a huge difference in people's lives. I am glad I decided to move forward with my passion.

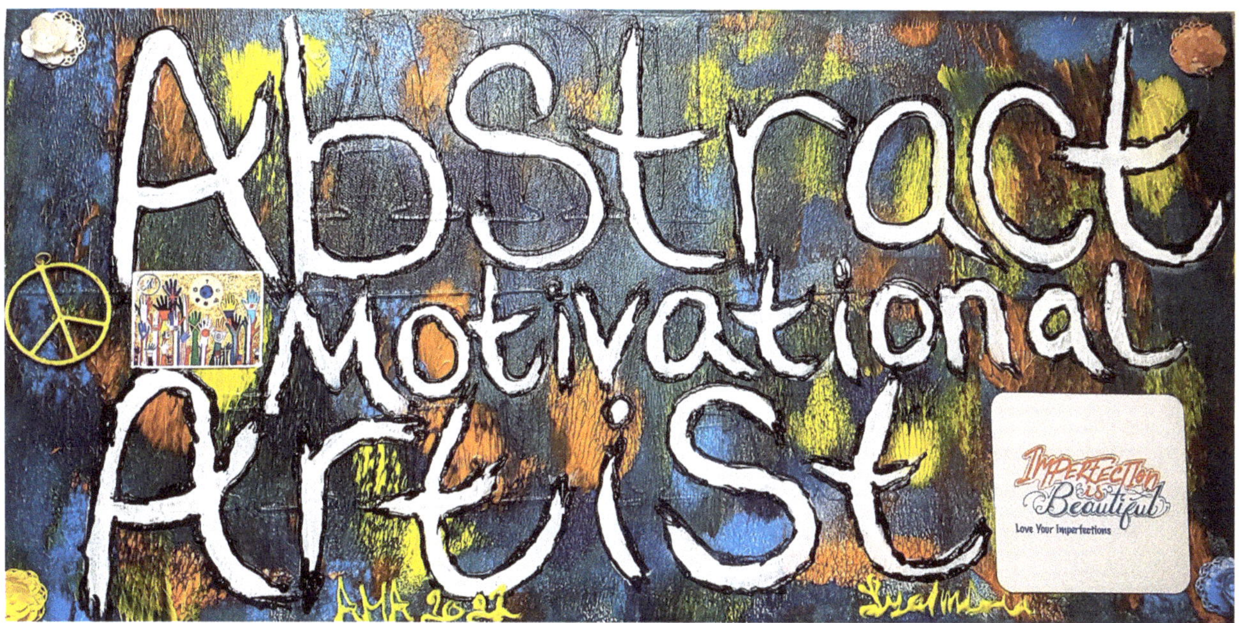

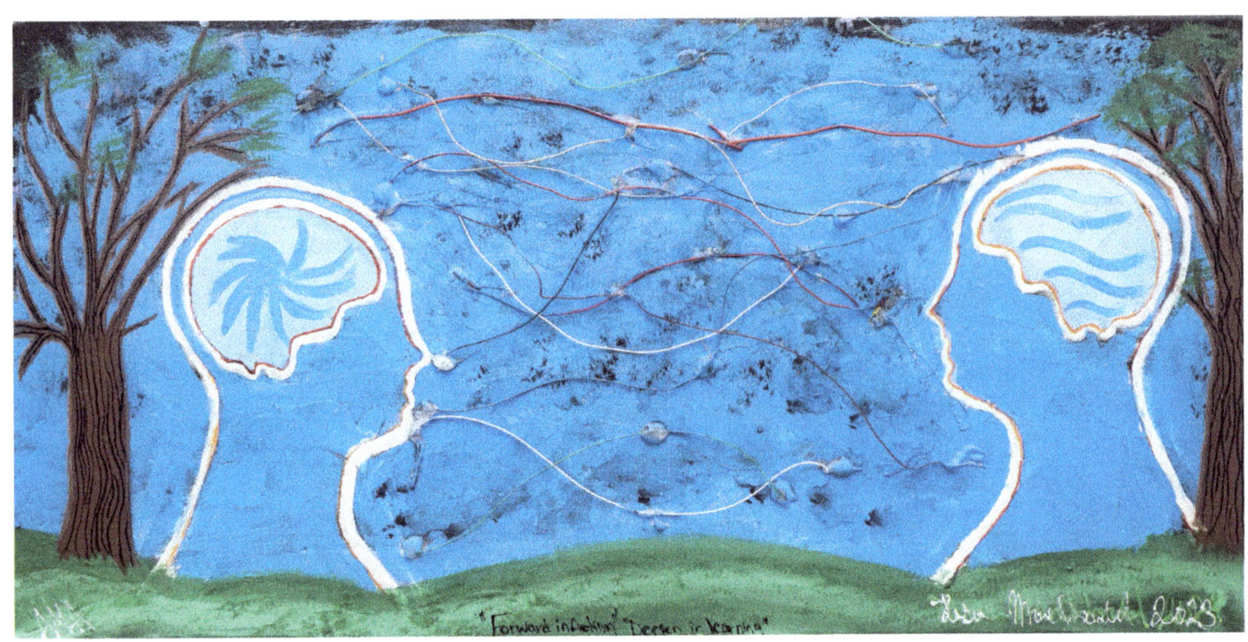

Motivational Life Coach

2022-2023

Adding more into my journey by owning *Imperfection is Beautiful* and being both an Abstract Motivational Artist and a Motivational Life Coach all connects and helps me to better understand youth minds. This is a huge transformation in my life, and it took me a bit to realize what works and what doesn't work in my business. I have been juggling a lot of things and trying to fit every puzzle piece together.

I realize that a lot of my art and motivational workshops consist of different themes but concentrate on self-discovery skills and coping skills. Then, I decided why don't I provide life coaching services that focus on self-discovery skills, coping skills, and time management skills. I added time management skills for people like me who have different ways of learning. I had to teach myself how to better manage my time during school.

I believe teens and young adults need a lot of guidance when it comes to time management skills. They also need self-discovery skills and coping skills. In our fast-paced world, a lot of young adults struggle with mental health issues. If we want youth to succeed, we need to teach them the proper tools to help them discover who they are and how to cope with life's issues.

I re-painted this painting, which I had originally created for my undergraduate art therapy degree project. I decided that the original looked too lost and not clear. I painted the whole background blue and added trees, grass, and swirls on both head silhouettes. I want my clients to feel these elements during our motivational life coaching sessions.

The left head silhouette represents my clients and how they are critically thinking on how they can get through their challenges. The right head silhouette represents me as a motivational life coach, and it shows how calm and collected I am when working with clients. The wires represent the exchange energy we are giving each other, which is helping us grow. The trees represent growth and strength between the client and the coach.

Redoing this painting gave me a sense of relief and enjoyment because I see my life much clearer now. I am now being true to myself.

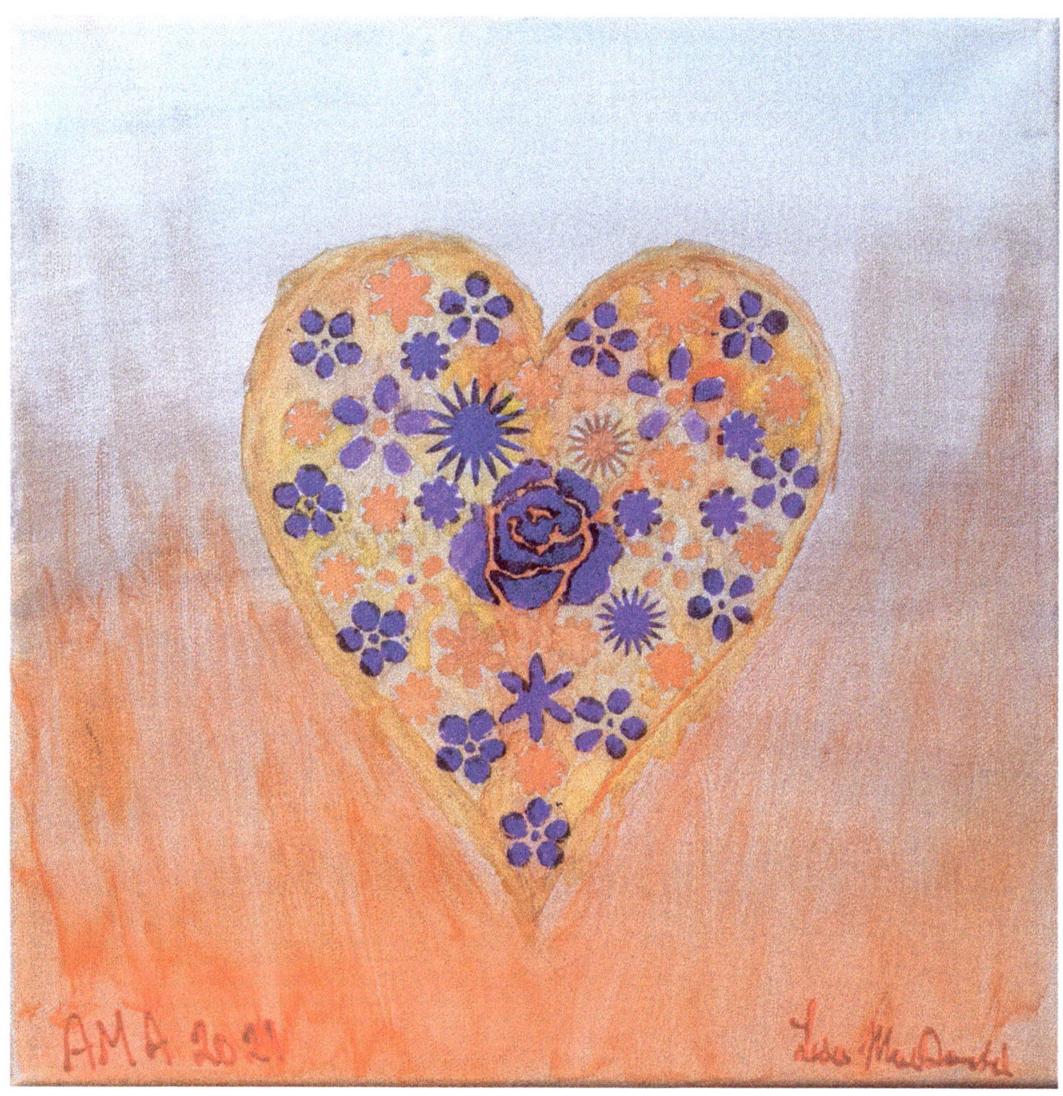

Abstract Motivational Artist Heart

2021

As an Abstract Motivational Artist, my goal is to create art that can connect and heal people. I decided to build my business up by creating Imperfection Is Beautiful LLC in April 2021. I took this step because I want people to take my business and art seriously.

In the summer of 2021, I received a grant from Allentown to do a coloring book workshop and give a motivational speech about accepting your imperfections in shelters. Winning that grant really boosted my confidence, making me felt like my work is making a difference and is valued.

This painting represents what it feels like to be an Abstract Motivational Artist. The orange and purple flowers indicate my emotions, such as excitement and appreciation.

Many people tell me they appreciate what I am doing. They tell me how much they used to let their imperfections hold them back.

I feel blessed to have a positive mindset and an outgoing personality—no matter how hard this world can be. The world needs more light than darkness, and with the heart I have as an Abstract Motivational Artist, I will keep shining that light out to the world.

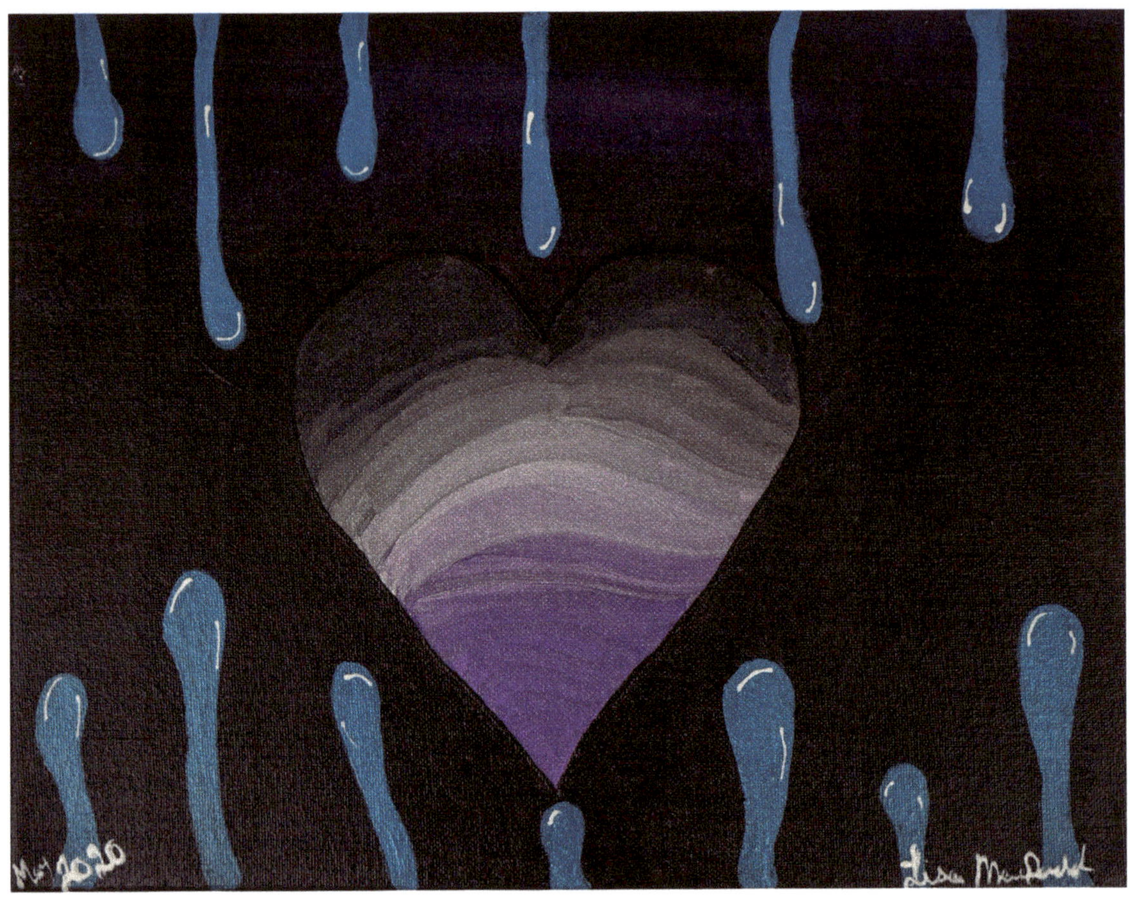

Faded

2020

I use my art to express both good time and hard times. When I look at this piece, it is very difficult to remember that I had to go through this experience. I had to let go of those tough feelings. I had to get them out and put them onto a piece of art.

This painting represents my experience being sexually harassed. I never thought I would be in that situation. But here I am, years later, still trying to get over the flashbacks and discomfort—feeling like I lost my inner strength.

That experience made me not want to be around with men. In fact, I just wanted to be alone in my room. I felt the darkness. Tears ran down on my face. I felt dirty and weirded out by what happened. It felt like the colors in my heart were fading away. There was no happiness left inside me. I kept having flashbacks over and over again. It made me depressed, not wanting to do anything.

That experience taught me to keep my guard up and to be more stern and serious. No one should face these types of situations, but we need to remember that we are strong-minded and that we can fight through this pain. We need to educate ourselves about self-defense and know how to protect ourselves from sexual harassment and assault.

The piece is called "Faded" because I felt weak, like I had lost my independence. When I completed this piece, it felt good. I had faced my emotions and projected what had hurt me onto this piece.

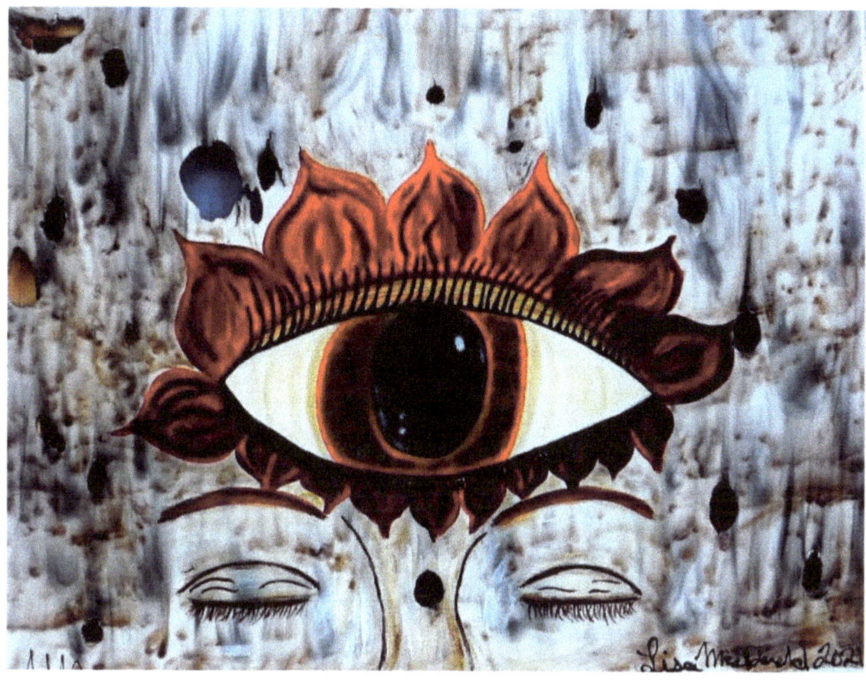

Third Eye Flame

2021

As I write, I am feeling a little better after from dealing with an intensive migraine. I get frequent migraines, which can be caused by hormones, weather changing, lack of sleep, not eating right, stress, anxiety, and allergies.

Most medications for migraine contain caffeine, which I'm unable to take because it gives me panic attacks during the day and insomnia at night. I don't like taking other pain medications because they make me nauseous. Who wants to feel nausea? I sure don't.

When I have a migraine, I can barely open my eyes and feel tremendous tension between my eyebrows. Migraines make me feel like my head is on fire, burning through my head. Some days when I have a migraine, I put icepacks on my head, and I'll go through four of them because my head gets really hot.

To prevent a migraine, before I go to bed, I meditate to help ease my mind and distract myself from negative thoughts. During one meditation, I had a vision of my third eye opening and popping out of my head. This third eye was a super vibrant, smokey orange.

They say when your third eye is open, you have a high sense of self, great deal of wisdom, and strong intuition. But when your third eye is unbalanced, you can have migraines, blurry vision, and sinus issues.

I painted this piece of the third eye that I saw in my meditation. I envision that my third eye is wide open and not letting me relax, it makes me want to close my eyes and not move, because more I move the more the eye will be wide open and go through this migraine again. When I have a migraine, it feels like my head is on fire and about to explode. It's very difficult to relax. I decided to burn this canvas to help my viewer understand the pain, heat, and pounding I feel. Seeing this painting reminds me to balance my my life and take my health more seriously to help decrease the migraines.

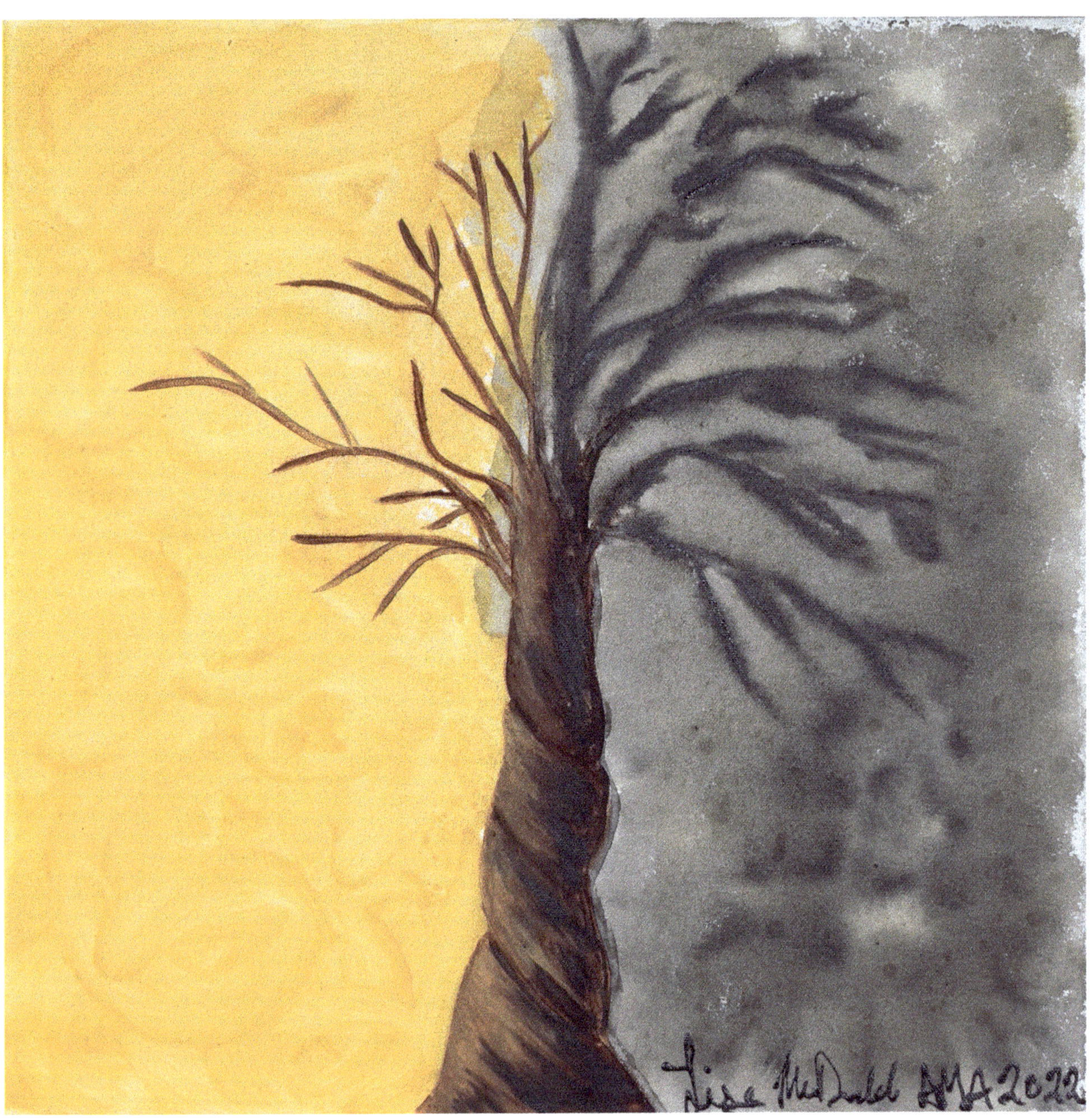

The Fear of the Unknown

2022

Fear can rob us from the ability to live our lives to the fullest. Sometimes we are scared to get outside of our comfort zone because we don't know what the result will be. We always want to predict what's going to happen, but life is not like that. We have to experience new things and learn from our mistakes. This helps us grow and become stronger.

I feel that there is a lot of unknown in life, and I am impatient to know the end result. I am a risk taker, and especially since 2017, I really stepped out of my comfort zone and put myself out there as an Abstract Motivational Artist.

I am also very future-focused, always wondering, *What will happen if I take this step? Will it hold me back? Or will I become more successful?* I question a lot of things in my life because I want to make sure everything I do is something that I can handle and be proud of. I know everything is not going to happen the way I want it to, and that's when I learn to accept those imperfections.

Every day, I wonder where I will go with my art and business. I constantly put myself out there and do my best to let people know all that I do. Questions pop into my head, *How can survive doing what I am doing? Will I be able to make a good amount of profit? Will I be able to afford my bills? Do I need to change my path?*

In 2022, I hadn't painted in a while, so I felt I needed to paint my feelings out. I painted this tree to represent myself as a strong, centered woman. I added warm tone on the left to represent the present moment. I added dark tone on the right with faded black branches to represent the unknown.

When I'm struggling with my fear of the unknown, I try to remember that I can't control the external world, but I *can* control myself and my actions. Yes, there is unknown, but if I try to use my time wisely and be productive, I will be more prepared for the future. If I ask the right questions, the answers will lead me where I want to go. I also need to be patient because things are not going to happen overnight. It's all just a process. I know I will get there someday.

Painting this tree made me feel good because I learned to let go and to know that no matter what happens, it's all opportunity to learn, grow, and get better! I know someday I will look back and think, *I am glad I didn't let my fears hold me back.*

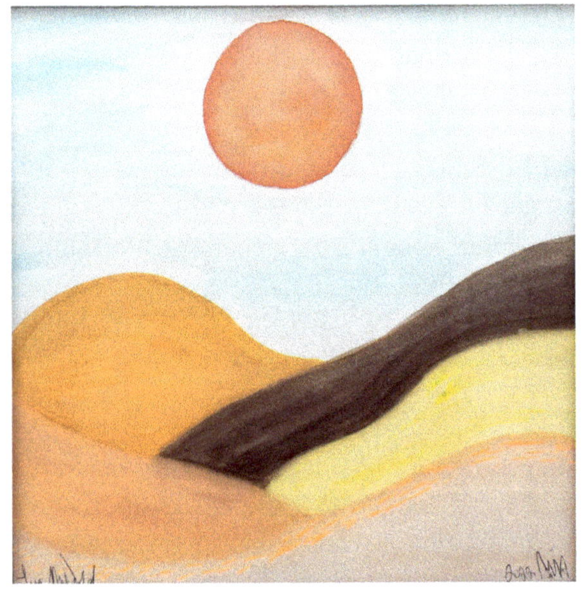 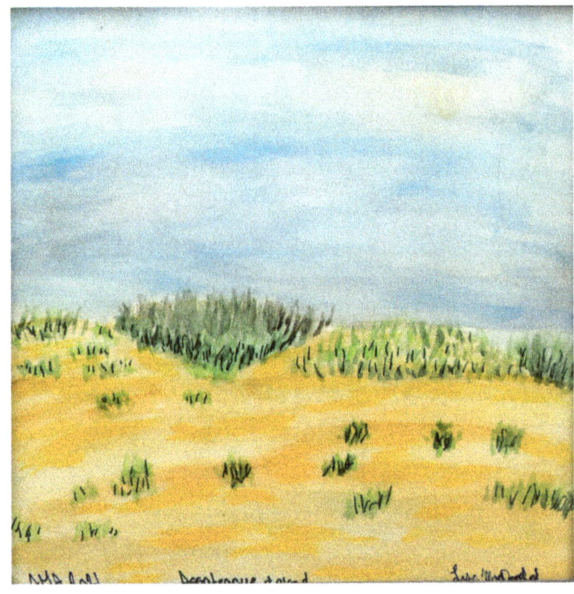

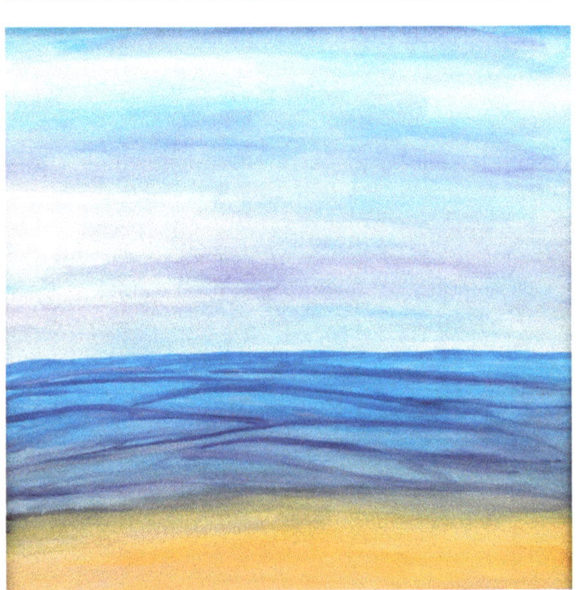 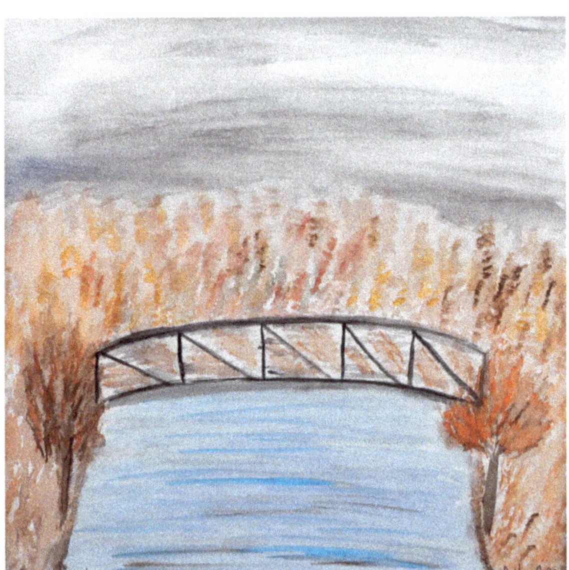

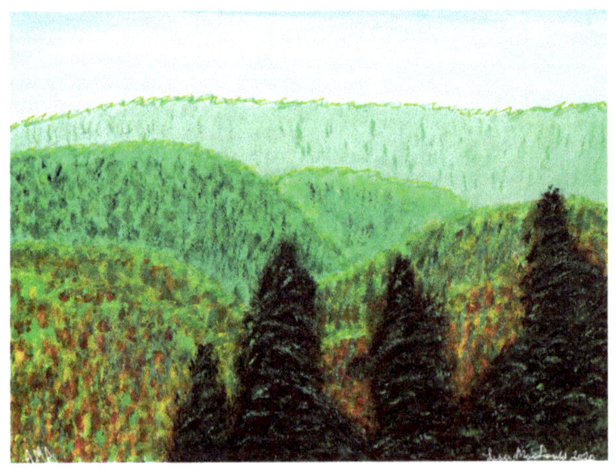

My Abstract View of Nature

2023

Being an artist, I have a unique mindset where I view the world differently than other people. When I was a little girl, nature was my best friend because when I was alone in nature, I wasn't being judged. I felt peace and quiet around me when I walked past the trees and was lying down on the grass. Everything was so still and peaceful! I wanted to stay there forever and not think about my challenges. I believe nature teaches a lot about life and how we should take care of it and be blessed by what it has for our human lives. Nature gives us a reminder to reflect on yourself and to be present with yourself.

My views in our world are always positive and colorful no matter how crappy people might act or how much negativity I hear from social media. Sometimes, it's hard to keep that perspective going, but when I spend time with nature the peace and happiness come back and I feel so alive. When I sit and stare at the view, I see every shape, color, movement, and sound as abstract and dramatic. I can envision the sounds in my head. It is a blessing that I can close my eyes and envision the natural world.

I see nature as a beautiful work of art. Everything pops with bright warm colors in the day, and toned-down colors at night. When I am outside in the daytime and listening to birds, I reflect on times spent in my grandmother's yard listening to those birds. It takes me back of my childhood, and the feeling I get is the painting *The Scent of my Childhood Life (see page 18)*. Everything just seem so colorful and happy when I am outside on spring and summer days.

During the night, I see dark tones of purples, blues, and dark greens. I get uncomfortable being in the dark, but when I practice seeing the goodness of being out in the night, it isn't bad just like the painting "Moonlight Shadows" on page 33. I love sitting outside at night and listening to crickets and watching the slow clouds drifting away with bright stars and moon shining through. I envision the night sky looking like Vincent Van Gogh's slow-moving strokes painting of the sky and the bright moon and stars.

I love how I paint nature. I don't create what I see in the real world, but rather what I envision and feel when looking at each aspect of nature. I see vibrant colors in abstract form where each plant, sun, grass, trees, water, animals, etc. have their own unique abstract look.

When I paint outside, I enjoy using watercolors because it flows nicely and blends beautifully. The watercolors allow me to flow imperfectly and create my own views of nature.

Nature is full of imperfections in shape, color, and form. I hope you connect deeply with my abstract nature paintings, to see yourself as beautiful and as imperfect as my imperfect nature paintings.

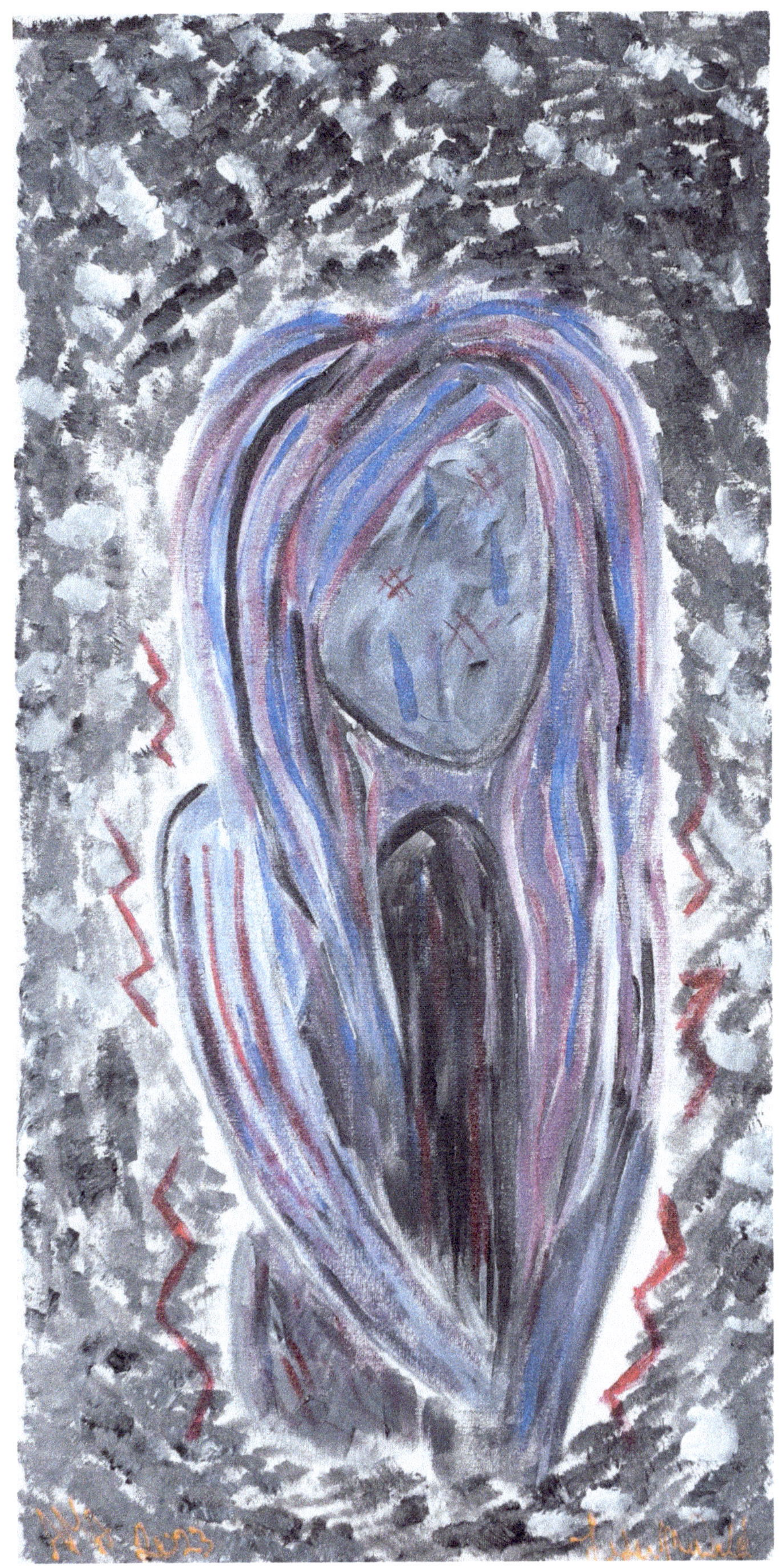

Going through Pain

2023

Going through mental and physical pain can be so draining. I have chronic pain. I feel it is important to be open about this—not because I want people to feel badly for me, but rather to let other people know they are not alone in their suffering.

Social media portrays so much perfection—but not many imperfections. No wonder so many people are anxious and depressed! We are constantly reminded that we need to live a perfect life—without any negative feelings. But we are human, and we have imperfect days.

When you are in pain, understand that just because you are in pain doesn't mean you are weak. You are strong because you are not giving up on yourself. You have the ability to ease this pain. Work with it, find what the main problem is, and be patient because it does take time to heal. If you need serious help, get the serious help you need and deserve now. Do not wait.

In my life, I've suffered with extreme migraines and menstrual pain. When I was recovering from my pain, I needed to express visually what I was going through. I was deeply sad because sometimes even I don't understand why I feel what I feel.

While I was painting this piece, I decided to use strong, messy brush strokes because pain is messy. I chose dark tones because when going through pain, people often feel like they are under dark clouds. I painted a female figure who is in a specific pose—the pose I do when I am in severe pain. I wrap myself together and fight the awful pain with tears and screams, not knowing when it will go away. I drew hashtag marks on the figure because even after the pain has gone away, it can leave a bad aching feeling afterward. It can be hard to move and do things because my body got traumatized through this pain and it needs extra time to heal.

When this painting was completed, I felt like I had released all of my sadness and mental and physical pain. I was ready to reconnect with myself and give myself some self-love. I am proud that I have not given up on myself and that I am strong enough to fight. While going through this process, I went out for a massage from a good friend of mine, Deb, who owns *Soul Body*. My gynecologist also referred me to physical therapy to calm my body and help me connect to my whole self. I am blessed that I am getting help. I know that everything will be okay.

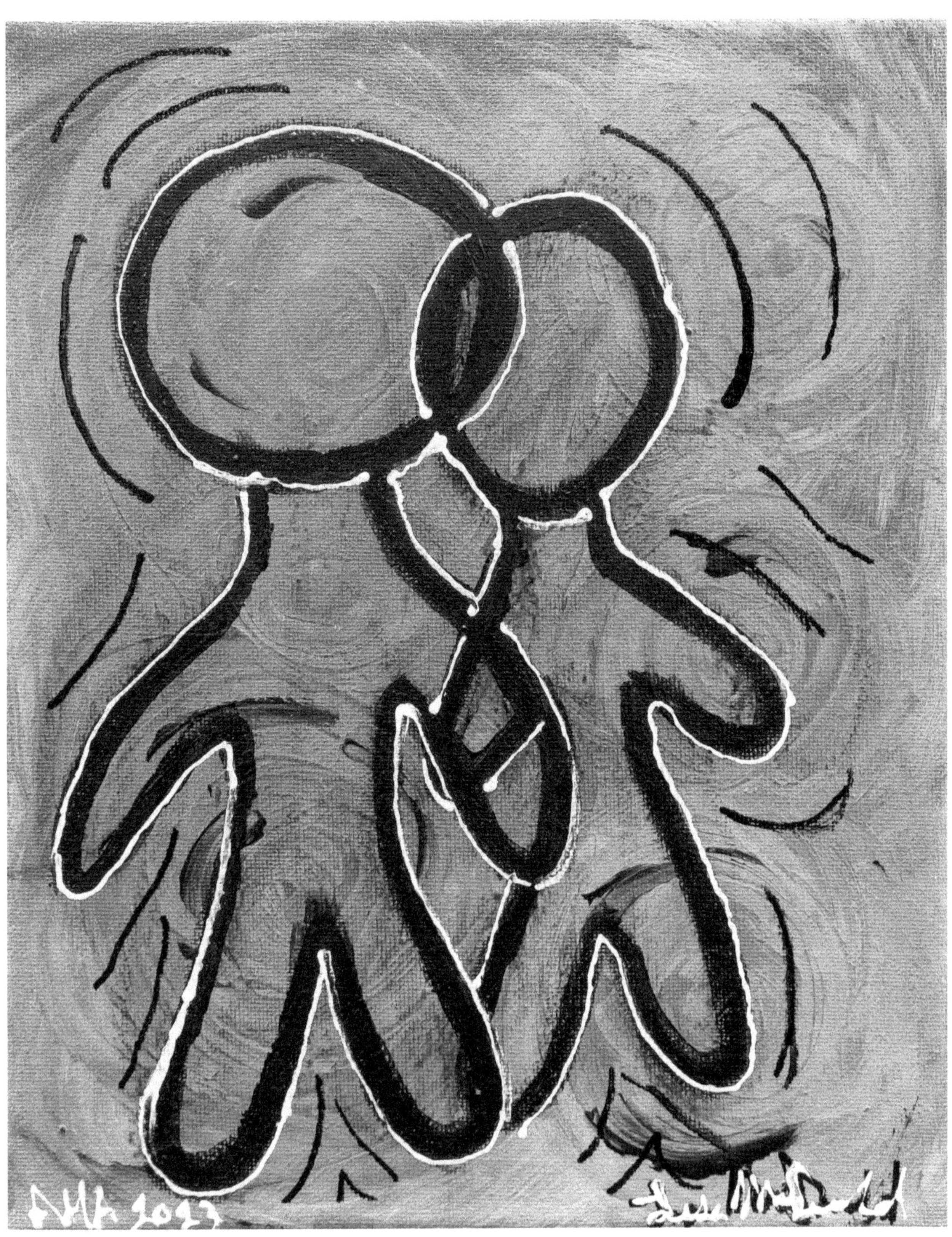

Feeling Disconnected from Myself

2023

I am very busy leading workshops, networking, working on my art, going to vending events, and so much more. I have been better managing my migraines. I make sure I drink enough water and protect myself during extreme colds and heat. I also make sure I eat well and stay consistent with my hygiene.

However, recently, I was experiencing crazy pain in my abdomen. It came and went, but on August 19, 2023, I felt it for twelve hours straight so I went to the emergency department. The doctor knew right away I needed surgery to remove my appendix. I was shocked!

I felt very uncomfortable not knowing how my body going to react to this. I like to be in control of my mindset, making sure I am good and thinking straight. When I got out of the hospital with a prescription for strong pain medication, I felt like I was entering into hell! It helped the pain, but it didn't help my mindset. I was freaking out, over thinking, and couldn't sleep. I was exhausted and losing my dang mind. I stopped taking the medication, and right away my body was sweating yet chilly at the same time. It was like going through a crazy withdrawal. I felt so disconnected from myself. It was like my mind was somewhere else and my body didn't know how to operate on it's own. It was the scariest thing ever!

I got a detox from a good friend of mine, Dr. Susan, and I followed her advice to help me get myself back together. And that it did! Little by little, I slept better, ate better, and thought better. It was like my mind and body were slowly conjoining back. I am forever grateful.

This painting represents the disconnection of myself when I go through chronic pain such as wisdom teeth surgery, migraines, menstral pain and now the appendix surgery. I made the body and head different sizes to show that there was no balance with my mind and body.

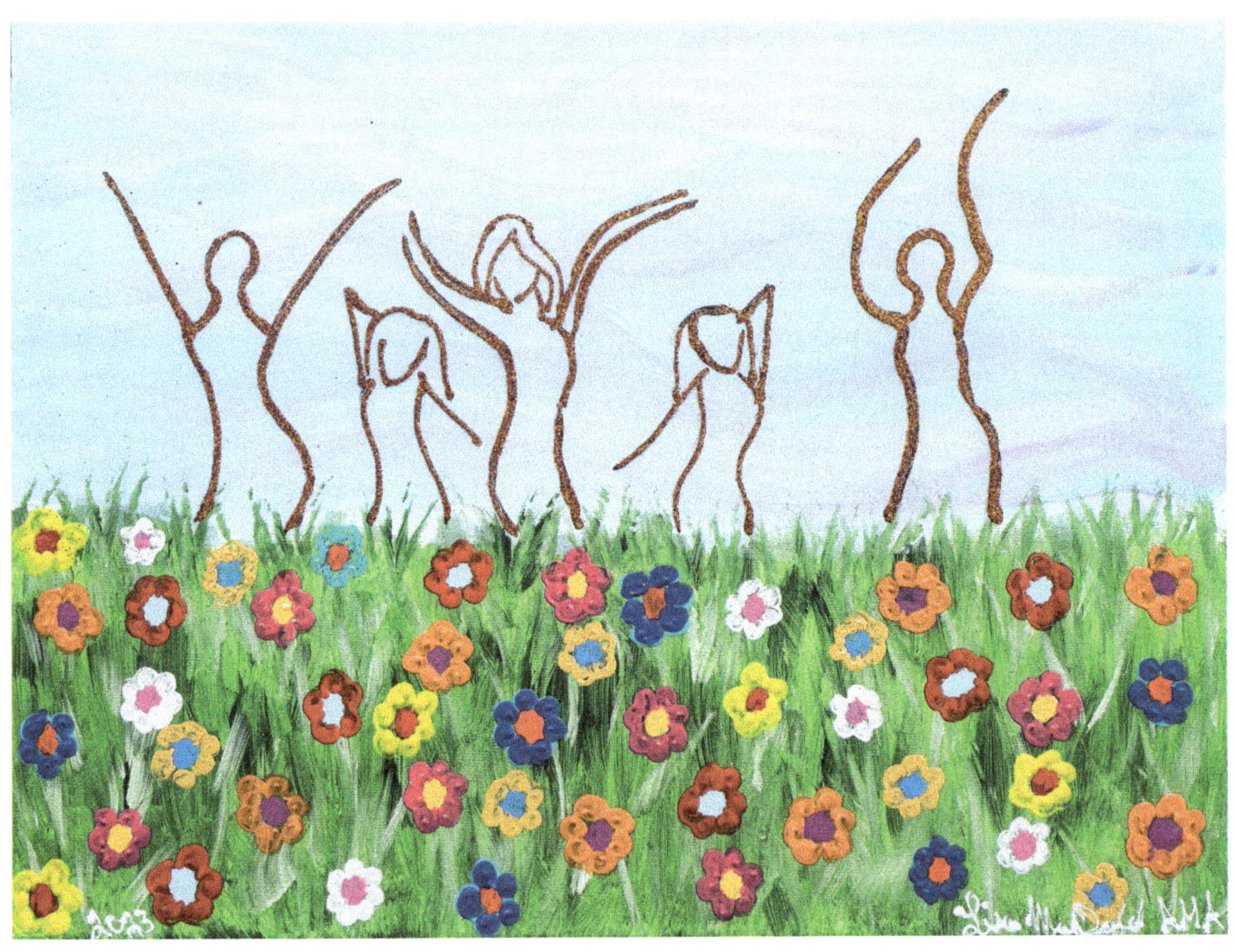

Feeling of Relief

2023

Going through this healing journey taught me a lot about life and health. As for life, it taught me to not take my family and friends for granted because having the support group that I have when going through this process was wonderful to experience. They cheered me on. As for health, I gained new knowledge about the mind and body and how to heal both. I was willing to learn because I didn't want myself to go into a deep dark path. I love myself so much and I know this world needs me more than ever! Every day, I make sure I keep my mind and body going positive no matter how exhausting it can be. Little by little I fight my everyday challenges to heal with knowledge and wisdom to help me get back together and to reconnect my mind and body.

In this painting, I wanted to capture feelings of relief through mental and physical sickness. As I embrace myself in nature, I see myself running in an open field filled with colorful flowers. The sunlight giving me the warmth and comfort and the flowers looking at me with rays of colors. This is the sense of freedom of not feeling anything at all. The sense of freedom, to be back to myself. I have learned so much from the darkness, and now the universe has congratulated me by providing me the sense of relief. I did my part by taking care of myself by following what my mind and body needs. It was hard because this was something new, I needed to learn to adapt, life always changes, nothing stays the same. I needed to teach myself to work with the imperfect flow of life. I do believe that we can't control our environment, but we can control our mindset. While working through this process, I have been working with my mind to help me view things clearer and become motivated to create a change.

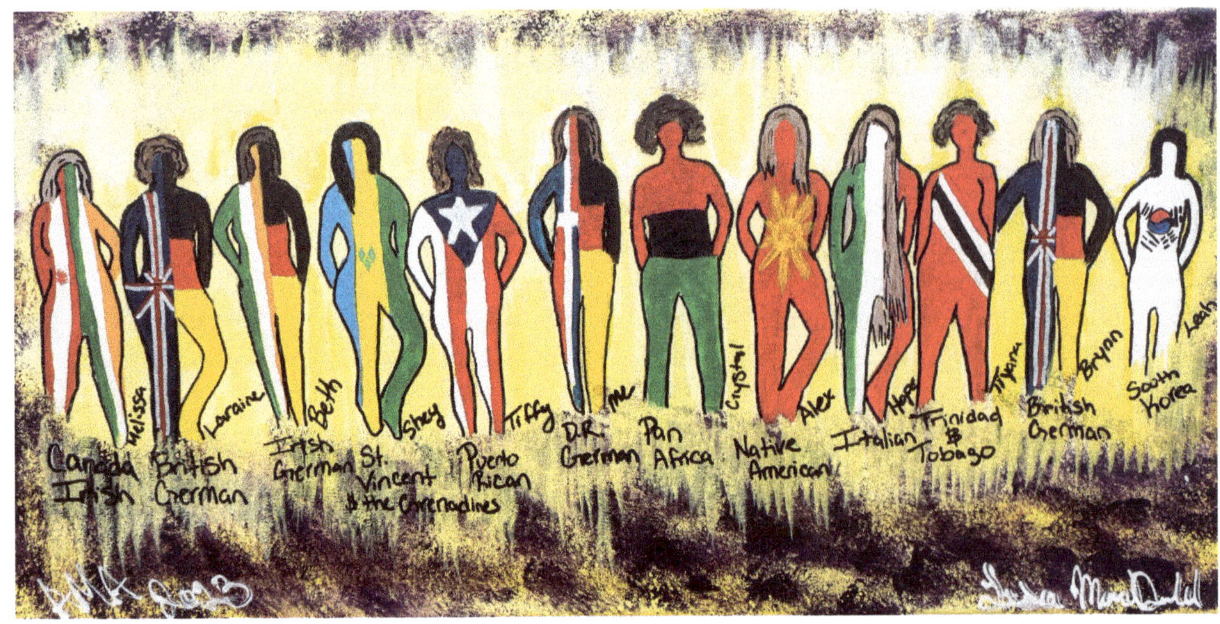

The Best Girlfriends I Could Ever Ask For

2023

In my life I had a hard time making friends, but through my difficult experiences and overcoming them made me get true loyal friends. The tough experiences I went through taught me to know when to have my shield up and to protect myself. I now know the signs of who is real and who is not real. I learned from my past and now allow good people into my life. It turns out I have the best girlfriends I could ever ask for!

The consistent support I have been receiving and amazing compliments are something I was not used too. I had to take a step back and stop putting the past front of me. I needed to allow myself to be present with these girls and see how much they listen to me and want to learn more about what I do. I felt no jealousy—only love and support. I want to express my gratitude to them and make sure they know that I really appreciate their presence.

The following are my closest friends. These women have known me from the worst times of my life to the best times of my life. They helped me fight for what was right for me, and they taught that I deserve respect and love. If I have a problem, they answer my calls and help me get through my tough times.

Leah: I have known this girl for years! We met when I was in second grade, and we were on the same bus. I always enjoyed sitting next to her because we always have a great conversation. I always see her as such a brilliant girl who isn't ashamed of her disability. She amazed me all the time, especially today. She has her struggles, but she makes things happen. She doesn't know how much of an inspiration she is. Leah is an unbeatable woman, who is working hard to pursue a degree in early childhood education, visit her wonderful boyfriend, and work on being independent. She is a fighter, and I respect that so much. She deserves so much in her life! I am blessed to have her as a great friend.

Brynn: I met this girl at our part-time job at a yogurt shop in 2018. The other girls there were a bit difficult to work with, but working with Brynn was different. She was fun to be around, and we had a great time working together. Today, we still go out to eat and talk about what is going on in our lives. We both help each other out, and we both laugh together about life's imperfect moments. She is very trustworthy friend, and I hope she knows I have her back.

Tiyana and Hope: I met Tiyana at my Mental Health Awareness Runway Show in 2022, and I met Hope in college in 2019, and she also attended the runway show. We three instantly connected in an inspiring moment. They sure knew how to work that runway show stage! I was inspired and proud to have them girls represent what I do in Imperfection is Beautiful.

Hope is a sweet quiet girl who does her own thing! I admire her talents kick boxing, nutrition, and modeling. She is a charming young lady.

Tiyana and I hit it off right after my runway show. She took it seriously, calmly, and confidently. She decided to be the first model to do the walk. I was so impressed and inspired. After the show, we stayed in touch and we met a couple times. We connected and spoke about our struggles to each other and see that we both can relate in different ways. When Tiyana gave birth to her beautiful baby girl named Girasol which means Sunflower in Spanish; I was there at her house as much as I could to help her with this little one. I want to help her as much as I can because I understand it can feel lonely to be with the baby.

For both Tiyana and Hope, I am sure we both can continue seeing each other and creating more memories. You both are amazing, don't stop believing in yourself and keep following what you truly love and believe in. I am doing it and so can you! You all have my support!

Alex: I have seen Alex around high school and always thought she hangs around with the cool people. We didn't speak until our high school reunion in 2018 I believe. When we connected, we instantly cried and laughed because we both thought the same thing about each other. We would talk for hours and it was inspiring to know who she really is.

Alex is a sweet woman who is open in the spiritual world. I have learned so much from her and she taught me how I am very open-minded into my spiritual world. She taught me how to be open with signs in my dreams, in my waking life, and through my art. We explore different spiritual traditions and being out with nature. We both enjoy our time being out with nature because it gives us a chance to get out of the reality world and being in beautiful nature. We express our concerns about the world, the people, nature, animals and much more. We can talk about all these things for hours because we both see it in the same perspective. She is just a fun and loving woman who she always has her arms open and welcomes me whenever I need some help. I am so grateful to have her as an amazing friend who I can connect with on a spiritual level.

Crystal: Oh this girl! I met her in high school art class 2014, she was a junior and I was a senior. I remember sitting right across from her in class along with other girls who were quite annoying. I was very quiet in art class because it was my favorite subject and I take this class more seriously than my other classes. I always thought that Crystal was like those annoying girls and I didn't want to get myself involved. When we worked independently, I remember talking to Crystal and thinking to myself that she isn't annoying like the other girls.

After I graduated high school, I remember we still stayed in touch, but I felt that we connected better a little after I started "Imperfection is Beautiful." When she got her degree in graphic design, we both collaborated and shared ideas. I found that her talent and how detailed she can get into a website and marketing items is incredible. She has the passion and it was beautiful to see. We both help each other to help improve our skills in our personal and professional lives.

Our friendship is getting stronger and stronger throughout the years. She is the type of woman I go to if I need a good laugh and to just get away from my chaotic life dealing with business stuff and the reality world; she helps me let go of all the tension and just be in the moment. We will spend hours talking, laughing out loud, and doing funny things. Crystal also is such a great helper, if I need help with my life coaching materials and need to practice, she is there to give me criticism, which will help me be better in my sessions. She also helps me with vending my art and merchandise, she is there assisting me and putting her heart and soul out there. I not only like to represent what I do, but when she is present with me, I love to tell my customer that she is the designer behind "Imperfection is Beautiful." This logo is going places and I want to make sure that Crystal's name goes out there too. Crystal deserves so much recognition because she is helping me live this dream life, and having a woman like her to help me is such a beautiful thing. I know that I have this amazing friend who not only helps me live my dream life as an artist, speaker, and a life coach, but who created a life-long friendship that is trustworthy. I will always keep our fun memories close to my heart and embrace every moment with her because she is a one of a kind friend!

Tiffy and Shey: Ah, these two amazing girls, I had seen them around in high school but never talked to them. Tiffy, I knew she was in the AP Art classes and she hung out with lots of the Hispanics and Shey was very quiet and I only seen her in my homeroom. I didn't really speak to both of them because I was dealing with a lot of drama with girls. I felt like I didn't need to try to be friends with others. I felt that I rather be alone than talk to another girl.

After high school when we all graduated in 2014, we all started to talk to each other, I don't remember how it all worked out but I knew Tiffy and Shey were hanging out often and it felt like they both opened their arms to include me in their friendship. It felt weird at first but the way they both are was so mature and it felt relaxing to chat with them. They are there to have fun and not to judge or hate one another. Tiffy, is very artsy and fashionable; whereas Shey is chill and the type to have fun who don't need the drama. Both together is like having my favorite ice cream chocolate with chocolate sprinkles and Oreo toppings. They were my kind of fun friends and it is something I needed especially with my worst nightmare of getting bullied in my senior year. When we all hang out, we love to go out to eat, go out to the bar and clubs, and have our ice cream. We can spend hours talking about our craziest stories where it has us laughing so much that our stomachs start to hurt. I always love spending time with these two girls, it brings me back to our teenage years no matter what age we are now. Tiffy and Shey will always be my two fun friends!

Beth: When I first moved in my home development, I got physically abused and mentally abused by the girls who live in there. I felt that I couldn't have a friend who can treat me fairly and just accept me. The only friend I made was my neighbors, Lester and JoAnn and then later they introduced me to Bethany. When I first met her in my early preteen years, I knew she was super country girl and seemed to want to have a fun and corky time. We sleep over at Lester and JoAnn's house and play funny games, do each other's makeup blindfolded. When we go out, we go to local country concerts, go to Cicis Pizza in Whitehall, and go to the mall into Clare's to try out different jewelry and just be silly. We also make sure we give company to JoAnn because we know she loves to have fun too. When spending time with Bethany it felt like I can be funny and silly without any hate. She meant a lot to me that I had her attend my Sweet 16 party and I had her sit with me at the horse carriage.

In our college years, we didn't see each other as much as before but we do stay in contact. Beth helped me a lot with college choices and deciding what can I do in my career path. During Covid 19, I was going through a crisis with how the world was becoming and how the college was being to me. I couldn't get counseling at that time and my accommodations was not being followed by the professor. When my art therapy professor was being so harsh to me, I needed to call Bethany after class. I cried so hard when I was on the phone with her, she listened and let me know that I have the right to do what is right for me. It felt so good to know that I have someone to have my back when I felt like the college itself didn't even care or acknowledge what I was going through.

As adults now, Bethany is teaching in elementary school inspiring kids to be the best that they can be! I am so happy to know someone who has passion in teaching and can make a difference for these little ones. She is going to not only make a positive impact to these children but make these kids have a brighter future. Bethany is a very hard-working woman because since her father passed away; she kept working hard in school and work. I know that is the most difficult thing to do, to continue even though you lost someone so close to you. However, a man came into her life just in time for her. She has such an amazing man who took her by her hand and gave her a lift. I am honored to be her maid of honor during her wedding day on July 2023 and able to experience her special moment. I cannot wait to see what more memories we can make together. Together we will make a positive impact to the youth.

Melissa and Laraine: My two powerful women here! While I have been networking and getting myself out there, I have met these two amazing women. First it was Melissa, I met her at Michael Madden Elite Networking event. All I can say I love her attitude; I love how straight-forward and to the point she is. She is an inspiring developmental life coach and everything she does is what I would love to do as a Motivational Life Coach. She is a great resource for me when I feel stuck on what I am doing with my Imperfection is Beautiful business. I admire her advice because I know she has a lot of experiences. As for my darling Laraine, I met her in LinkedIn. I just saw her profile and what she does was similar to what I was doing in my workshops. We connected instantly and became close friends. I see Laraine more as an aunt to me because she has such a warm heart and soul where she helps me make the right choices. She supports me at my events and enjoy every idea that I come up with. She is an incredible editor; she helps me with my motivational documents/speeches. She always says how much wisdom I have for such a young age.

When I was going through sexual harassment at a job, I felt like I didn't have a voice and I felt like I needed to meet with them both in person and discuss about my issues in the job. Laraine and Melissa felt that this needed to be taken more seriously and that I needed to do something right away. Melissa said, "Let's get your stuff and leave that place," and Laraine was following along and agreed that it is something I needed to do. Speaking to them felt good and made me feel like I had a voice to be heard. Melissa came out of her way to follow me to go to that job to help me grab my stuff and we both just left. This was the most anxiety provoking experience I have ever gone through in my entire life. That day I learned that I need to stand my ground and speak up, because if not, I will get taken advantage of. I am so happy that I left this job because it gave me the opportunity to explore more in my Motivational Life Coaching business. Melissa and Laraine have taught me so many meaningful lessons in my life. We all work as a great team that we call our team the Dream Team. We all are doing something for each other and for our community. I am grateful to know that I will always have ongoing support from these two ladies. They both believe in me so much that it motivates me to keep on striving!

I wanted my painting to represents how diverse my friends are by painting their flags on each of their body image. While being friends with each of them, I learned so much about them, where they are from, their traditions, their foods, their cultures and so much more. In this painting, I want my viewers to see this painting as if it was me viewing these women. It is my vision of what I see in my women in an abstract way. I want to include them to be all different in their own ways. As their own ways, I painted them in all different body image. I want to demonstrate on the painting that we all have different body image and it should be embraced not be ashamed. I know some women struggle with their look, but when I am friends with someone, I embrace everything about them because they deserve to feel beautiful. I love seeing all of us embracing each other as beautiful imperfect women. It's what I have always dreamed of since I was a little girl. I want to be the one in my friend group to show them that they can love their true natural self because we are humans and we are meant to look beautifully imperfect. There is nobody like my best girlfriends.

About the Author

Lisa is the founder of Imperfection is Beautiful, which represents Lisa and her work of art. Lisa calls herself an Abstract Motivational Artist because she is an artist and a motivational speaker. As an artist, she creates nationality and motivational paintings. Her purpose for the paintings is to help make others feel good and give them a reminder to never give up.

She found that her paintings are a helpful way to work through her emotions and to help others too. This is where her company started because she wanted to help motivate others through her paintings and workshops. She began to do this by providing others with art activities, motivational speeches, workshops, and coaching.

As a motivational speaker, she speaks to people about how to accept their imperfections and how to have a strong mindset when going through difficult times. She also offers workshop programs that are based on art activities and motivational speeches. In her private sessions, she offers certified life coaching skills that focus on personality discovery, coping skills, and time management skills.

Lisa MacDonald has done motivational speaking in East Penn School District. She was the keynote speaker for the Mental Health Awareness Walk, and she has done her first seminar called "The Power of Imperfections."

She graduated from Lehigh County Community College and earned her bachelor's degree in arts at Cedar Crest College.

Thank you for reading my book!

I hope that my art and story inspire you to share your own to help spread awareness that we are never alone in our challenges.

Don't be ashamed of your imperfections. Embrace them! Speak about them and let other people know that they can push through their challenges too!

We are all here for a reason! Be that reason and live your dream life!!

- Follow me in my imperfect journey through social media:

- Facebook: www.facebook.com/abstract.motivational.artist

- Instagram: Imperfection_is_Beautiful17

- Art Instagram: AbstractMotivationalArt

- TikTok: Motivationallifecoach

Own Lisa's Art

Prints of all of the art featured in this book are for sale in a wide range of sizes, including 5X7, 8X10, 9X12, 11X14, and 16X20. Contact lisamacdonald936@yahoo.com to order

---

Imperfection is Beautiful

Love Your Imperfections

EMPOWERING THE COMMUNITY THROUGH ART AND MOTIVATION PROGRAMS

Self-Love Program: This program is designed to help women cultivate a strong sense of self-worth, build self-esteem, and gain inner peace. In each workshop, participants will be guided through art and motivation speaking.

Middle and High School After-School Program: This program consists of 13 weeks of art activities, motivational speaking, and group activities. This benefits youths' communication skills, build self-esteem, and leadership skills.

Veterans Workshops: These art expression workshops contain different themes and art materials. Each veteran will have the opportunity to express themselves visually and open up in a safe space.

Motivational Life Coaching Servies

- Self-discovery skills

- Time management skills

- Coping skills

For More Information
484-619-3461
LISAMACDONALD936@YAHOO.COM
TikTok: Motivationallifecoach
FB: Abstract motivational artist
IN: Imperfection_is_beautiful17
Art IN: Abstract_Motivational_Art
Etsy:Imperfectionbylisa
www.imperfectionisbeautiful.life